Artful Appliqué

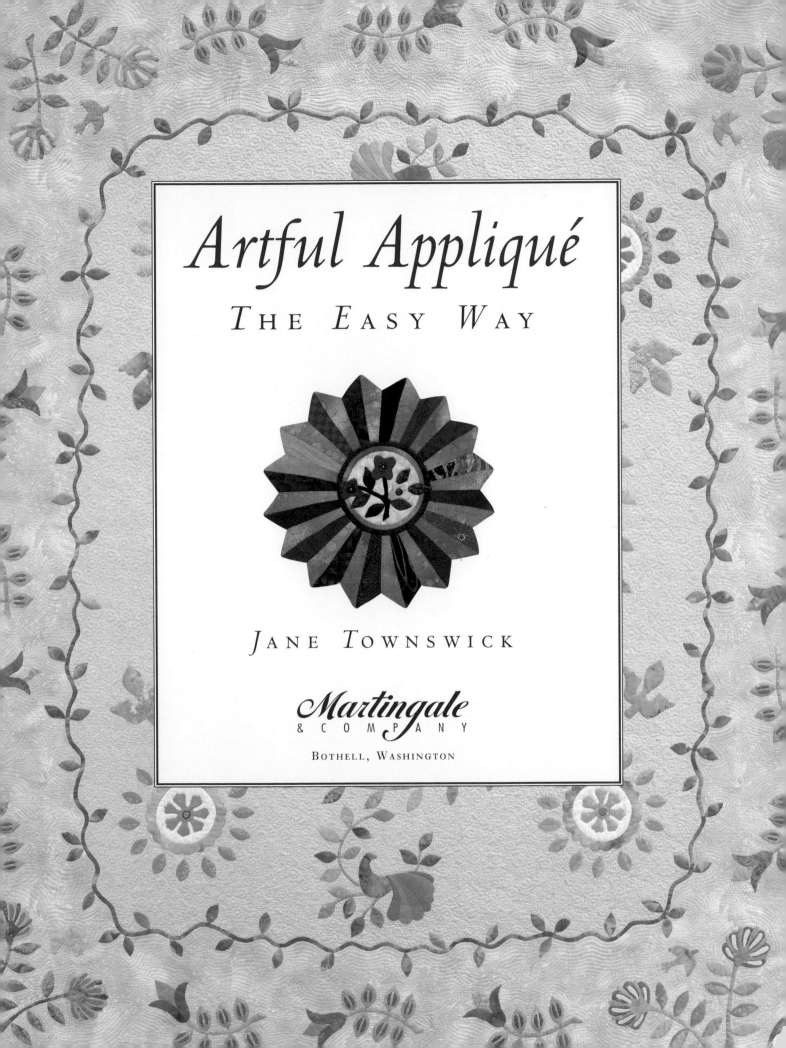

Artful Appliqué

The Easy Way

Jane Townswick

Martingale
& COMPANY

Bothell, Washington

Credits

President . . . . Nancy J. Martin
CEO/Publisher . . . . Daniel J. Martin
Associate Publisher . . . . Jane Hamada
Editorial Director . . . . .Mary V. Green
Technical Editor .Ursula Reikes
Copy Editor . . . . .Tina Cook
Design and Production Manager . . . . Stan Green
Cover and Text Design . . . . .Trina Stahl
Illustrator . . . . Laurel Strand
Photographer . . . . Brent Kane

Artful Appliqué: The Easy Way
© 2000 by Jane Townswick

Martingale & Company
PO Box 118
Bothell, WA 98041-0118 USA
www.patchwork.com

That Patchwork Place is an imprint of
Martingale & Company.

Printed in China
05 04 03 02 01 00   6 5 4 3 2

Library of Congress Cataloging-in-Publication Data

Townswick, Jane.
    Artful appliqué : the easy way / Jane Townswick.
       p. cm.
    ISBN 1-56477-294-2
      1. Appliqué—Patterns. 2. Patchwork—Patterns.
      3. Quilting—Patterns. I. Title.
    TT779.T69 2000
    746.46'041—dc21   00-022293

Mission Statement

We are dedicated to providing quality products and service by working together to inspire creativity and to enrich the lives we touch.

DEDICATION

To my students, the real authors of this book

ACKNOWLEDGMENTS

*I am grateful to Steve Carr, owner of the Summer House Needleworks shop in Oley, Pennsylvania,
for allowing me to teach appliqué classes in the most creative and inspiring environment
any quilter could ever imagine.
Many thanks to all the people who allowed their quilts to be shown
in the photo gallery of this book. I'm also grateful to Brent Kane, for taking such beautiful photographs.
And my **utmost** gratitude to my editor, Ursula Reikes, whose sense of clarity
and careful attention to detail made this a better book.*

Contents

Introduction

**A**S THE OWNER of Quilter's Cupboard in Rockford, Illinois, from 1987 to 1990, I had the chance to attend local, regional, and national quilt shows where I could see some of the world's most beautiful quilts. Having been a die-hard patchwork fan for many years, I thought there was very little reason for appliqué quilts to exist—until Nancy Pearson's "Techny Chimes" quilt stopped me dead in my tracks. Her composition and use of color were masterful. It was this breathtakingly beautiful image that sent me on an immediate and frenzied quest to find the nearest person who could teach me to appliqué.

My fascination with fine hand stitching continued as I traveled to the International Quilt Market and Festival in Houston each fall. In 1988 I was lucky enough to attend a class taught by appliqué expert, artist, and scholar Elly Sienkiewicz. The class was based on the designs from her book *Spoken without a Word*. Elly's wonderful techniques and patient encouragement made me believe I could actually become skilled at hand appliqué. Over the next two years I continued to enjoy her classes and started to develop my own designs, and classes for my shop.

In 1990 I entered into a career in publishing, first at Chitra Publications' *Traditional Quiltworks*, *Quilting Today*, and *Miniature Quilts* magazines, and later at Rodale Press as a quilt book editor. My experience as an editor gave me an even greater appreciation for the work being done by quilt artists all over America.

Gail Kessler, owner of the Summer House Needlework shop in Oley, Pennsylvania, gave me the chance to teach classes based on my designs in 1997, for which I will always be grateful to her. Since then, Steve Carr, the shop's present owner, has continued to make me welcome. I was eager to teach classes because I wanted to give my students reliable techniques that they could use in any appliqué project. Where precision was important, I taught ways to match angles and points, align leaves on branches and vines, create perfect ⅛"-wide bias strips, and more. Where precision was less important, such as in the direction leaves fell, or in the way flowers curved, I showed students how to let their own preferences take over and allow the design to reflect their inner sensibilities. Putting your individual stamp on an appliqué design is a natural process that creates artful results.

My students' enjoyment and stitching success inspired me to write this book. Look through the photo gallery (pages 21–33) to see the creativity and beautiful workmanship in their quilts. Notice the different ways blocks are set together, and the varied color palettes that make each quilt an artistic expression of its maker. Can you find the innovative extra touches and surprise elements that many people added—a dewdrop on a lily, a wreath design expanded into a whole quilt setting, vines that emerge from a block to become an entire border treatment? Look for quilts that feature all sixteen block designs, and others that use just a few, or only one. See what happens when you use a technique, such as perfect bias strips, to surround leaves and flower petals with dramatic ⅛" bands of color.

The designs and techniques in this book follow in order from simple to increasingly complex. Start with the easier ones and progress to the more intricate blocks. Use each chapter as a way to learn appliqué methods that will give you greater stitching success, and as a source of ideas for developing your own artful impulses. When you reach the final block, Twining Lily, you'll be able to tackle any appliqué project you like—and stitch it *your* way.

Jane Townswick

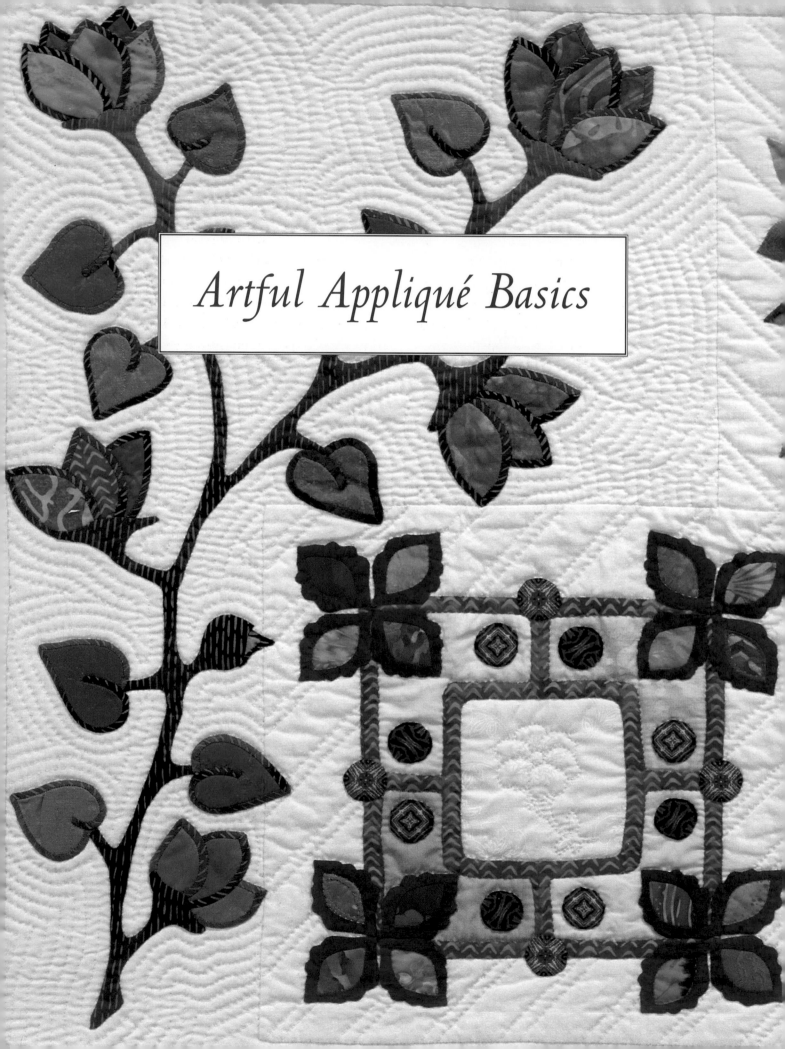

Artful Appliqué Basics

**B**EAUTIFUL HAND APPLIQUÉ is as individual as a fingerprint. It comes from combining colors and fabrics that please you, choosing designs that appeal to you, and using techniques that produce results you like. With each new block in this book, you'll learn reliable appliqué methods, including easy unit appliqué, appliquéing without templates, and my own method for making perfect bias strips with a hera marker. Best of all, there is no need to mark background fabrics—except for marking occasional permanent placement lines.

Fabrics and tools that produce good results make hand appliqué more enjoyable. The following pages list the things I count on to give me stitching success every time.

Fabrics

TODAY'S broadcloth-weight, 100 percent cotton fabrics are wonderful for hand appliqué. They're easy to mark, stitch, and press, and we have more colorful and beautiful fabrics to choose from than ever before. One of the first things you'll notice about the instructions in this book is that the fabric lists don't specify colors. In each block, you'll find information about the way I use color. You can follow my example or make your own choices.

Look at the quilts in the photo gallery (pages 21–33), and notice how different the same block looks when done in different fabrics. You're almost sure to conclude that leaves really don't have to be green! Let your imagination make the rules for

Cottons and silks

you—if you want to appliqué a purple tree, a lime-green bird, or pink, gold, blue, and orange leaves, your quilts will only be more beautiful because of your creative touch. There's freedom in throwing away long-standing color "rules" and stitching something purely for fun.

In addition to today's wonderful cottons, try some of the following fabrics in your next block.

BATIKS

Because they are closely woven, batiks don't fray or ravel easily. This makes them a great choice for tricky shapes like steep points, narrow openings, and deep inner curves. And the gorgeous printed batiks now available are like having a fabric "paint box" at your fingertips.

SILK DOUPPIONI

For adding a lustrous sheen and interesting visual texture to any appliqué shape, silk douppioni is the ultimate choice. Interface the wrong side with a very lightweight, fusible tricot interfacing to stabilize the fabric and minimize fraying while you stitch.

HAND-PAINTED COTTONS

Any appliqué design will become one of a kind when you use hand-painted fabrics. My favorites for stitching flowers, birds, and leaves are Micky Lawler's Skydyes fabrics. Each of these is a work of art, and no two are ever the same (which means I'll never have enough). You can find beautiful hand-painted fabrics from many talented artists at regional and national quilt shows, at your local quilt shop, and sometimes in mail-order catalogs.

Batiks and hand-painted fabrics

Supplies

BECAUSE quiltmaking is such a creative process, it's always fun and exciting to search for better tools and supplies. Try some of the following and see if you like them. For more information about these products, refer to "Resources" (page 141).

TEMPLATE MATERIALS

Freezer paper is easy to mark, fold, and cut accurately, which makes it a great template choice for stems, branches, and flower petals. It's also a convenient option for shapes that occur only once or twice in a design. The waxy side of freezer paper presses easily onto fabric, and templates can be kept and reused until they no longer stick.

Lightweight template plastic is strong, and easy to mark and cut. Its sturdy nature makes it ideal for repeated shapes, such as leaves.

CIRCLE STENCIL

You can find plastic circle stencils in office- and art-supply stores. These rectangular pieces of plastic contain circle openings of many different sizes. They're easy to use and more accurate than cutting circle patterns.

MARKING PENS AND PENCILS

Pigma Permanent Marking Pens

Pigma pens work very well for marking appliqué shapes onto light and medium-colored fabrics. The .01 millimeter pen produces thin, easy-to-see lines that won't smudge or smear—just remember to keep the pen moving evenly over the fabric. When you use a Pigma pen, the permanent lines won't bleed into the fabric or be visible after your stitching is complete.

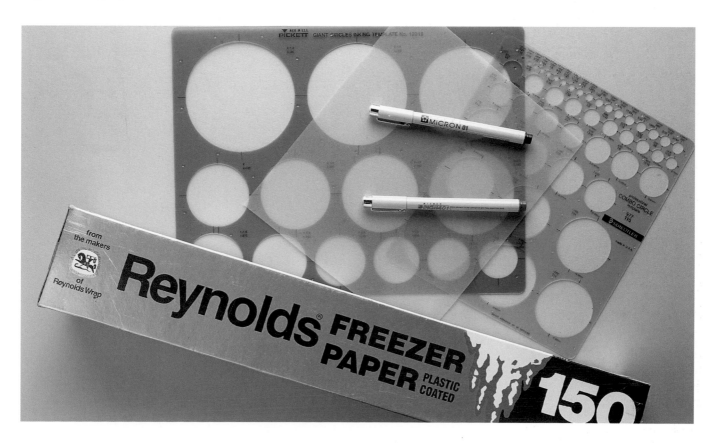

Pentel Milky Gel Rollers

If you haven't used a Pentel Milky Gel Roller pen on dark fabrics or busy prints, you may be in for a nice surprise. These pens come in white and several other light colors, and they glide over fabric as easily as Pigma pens. The ink is permanent and will not smudge or smear. Not much is known about long-term effects of these marking tools on fabric, however, so this is something to consider carefully if you're concerned about what may happen to a quilt after many years.

Marking Pencils

Silver and white marking pencils are always reliable for marking appliqué patterns on fabric. The tips stay sharp for a long time. These pencils are also great for marking quilting designs.

Sharpie Markers

Sharpie permanent markers are good choices for marking appliqué shapes on both freezer paper and template plastic because they create lines that won't smudge or come off on your fingers.

SCISSORS

Small, sharp-to-the-tip embroidery scissors are vital for beautiful hand appliqué. My favorite is a 3½" pair of Gingher embroidery scissors. I use them to clip narrow seam allowances along inner curves and deep inner points, and to trim fabric around steep outer points. They always make clean, crisp cuts and never seem to wear out.

Whenever you're looking for a new pair of scissors, try different brands. Ask for a piece of scrap fabric and test each pair to see which scissors cut cleanly and feel best in your hand.

Threads

Today there is a wider array of threads than ever before—so many that it's possible to match almost any fabric exactly. To make sure your stitches are invisible, always match thread color to appliqué shapes.

One-Hundred Percent Cotton

Mettler Silk Finish, DMC 50, and Gütermann cotton are wonderful threads for hand appliqué, and they come in so many luscious colors you'll probably want to own a spool of each color that is available!

Silk

Silk thread is so smooth that it almost seems to melt into the fabric. You can find a wide range of colors from TIRE and YLI. Look for taupe, gray, and coral shades—these will work well on many different fabric colors. If you like using silk douppioni, try appliquéing it with silk thread for the ultimate stitching experience. Cut silk thread in short lengths to help avoid fraying and tangling.

Beeswax and Thread Conditioner

Repeatedly pulling a strand of thread through fabric can make it twist, creating tangles and hard-to-undo knots. Coat a length of thread with natural beeswax or a synthetic thread conditioner, such as Thread heaven, to keep it tangle-free and easy to use.

Needles

Straw Needles

The size of your hand is the best guide for deciding which needle you'll enjoy using for hand appliqué. If you have long, slender fingers, you may like the length of a #11 Straw Needle from Foxglove Cottage (see "Resources" on page 141). I

like these needles very much, because they're long enough that I can keep my fingers out of the way while I work. That makes it easy to see exactly where to insert the needle for every stitch.

Sharps

If your hands and fingers are short or small, try using another of my favorite needles, the #12 Sharp from Hapco Products (see "Resources" on page 141). If there is a more delicate, thinner needle anywhere, I've never found it. This needle has such a thin shank that it glides through fabric almost without leaving a hole.

Needle Threaders

It can be difficult to thread fine needles, so I use a Clover double needle threader to thread both #11 Straw and #12 Sharp needles.

Thimbles

You may want to wear a thimble on the finger you use to push the needle. Finding a thimble that feels comfortable is important. Thimbles that have a raised edge around the top are great for catching a needle before it slips. If you don't like the feel of any kind of thimble, try using a suede Thimble Pad. These little circles have adhesive on the back that make them stick to your fingers.

Pins

Small, thin straight pins help keep even the tiniest appliqué shapes in position on a background square. Sequin pins are available in ½" and ¾" lengths, and Clover offers sequin pins with white heads, making them easy to spot in carpeting or upholstery. Try silk pins, which are long, with thin shanks that don't leave large holes in fabric. Experiment with different types and brands of pins to see which are your favorites.

Wooden Toothpicks

I can't be without a wooden toothpick for doing hand appliqué. My favorites are made of bamboo. They are strong, with sharp tips that easily turn under even the narrowest seam allowances. High-quality toothpicks are available in grocery stores, restaurants, and hardware stores. You'll like the way they help you create smooth curves and sharp points. Look for short and longer toothpicks and experiment by using both to decide which length you prefer.

Hera Marker

The perfect bias technique I've developed requires the use of a hera marker. This plastic tool has a curved shape and a sharp edge at one end for scoring perfectly straight lines on fabric. Many quilt shops sell or can order heras. I like to keep at least a couple on hand, in case I misplace one.

Rotary-Cutting Equipment

For some appliqué shapes, templates aren't even necessary. In these instances, you'll need a rotary cutter and cutting mat, quilter's rulers (1" x 6" and 3" x 18" are good choices), and a hera marker. A 9½" or 12" square ruler is helpful for squaring up blocks after your appliqué is complete. In addition, one of my favorite tools is the Salem Folding-Square, a jointed ruler that's great for making large appliqué blocks. The ruler unfolds to form a 90° angle, making it possible to cut accurate squares up to 24". Using the Folding-Square in conjunction with a 12" square ruler allows you to accurately center a design within a square.

Getting Started

IN THIS SECTION, you'll learn how to gain perfect control over needle and thread, as well as how to start and end a line of stitching invisibly. You'll also learn how to make tiny appliqué stitches, which will help you create fluid curves and sharp points.

Anchoring a Needle and Thread

The first step to stitching success is gaining control over your needle and thread. Beaders and silk-ribbon embroiderers use a trick that works beautifully.

1. Thread a needle with an 18" strand of thread. Holding the needle in your right hand, pick up the short end of the thread between your left thumb and index finger. Lay the thread over the fingernail of your left index finger, bringing it around your finger, and grasp the longer part of the thread together with the short end.

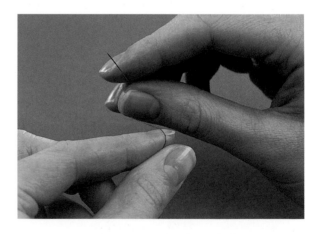

2. With the needle in your right hand, hold the threads in your left hand tightly so that the thread stays taut across your left index fingernail. Point the tip of the needle at the thread. Slide the needle across the surface of your fingernail so that the tip of the needle just pierces the thread; then immediately stop pushing the needle.

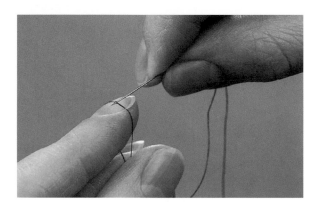

3. Pick up the needle *tip* with your left hand, and gently pull the thread down along the shank of the needle with your right hand. This will lock the thread securely onto the eye of the needle. This is *not* a knot. When you anchor a needle onto a thread in this way, you'll be in complete control of the needle and thread as you stitch. The needle will stay in the same place on the thread until you release it. You won't ever lose another needle, and you'll be able to work with more of the actual thread length, because the needle is anchored close to the short end of the thread.

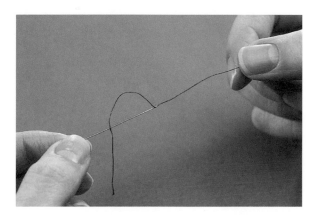

4. To change thread, simply pull gently on the short end of the thread.

5. Make a small quilter's knot at the long end of the thread. Hold the needle and the long end of the thread together in your right hand. With your left hand, gently wind the thread twice around the needle, and slide the wound threads down the shank of the needle so that they lie between your right thumb and forefinger.

6. With your left hand, pull the needle out from between your fingers without letting go of the wound portion. This will slide the wound portion down the entire length of thread and create a small knot at the end.

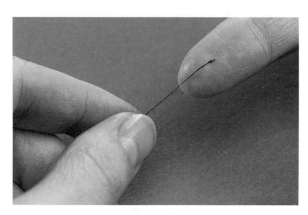

MAKING TINY APPLIQUÉ STITCHES

1. After anchoring a strand of thread on a needle and knotting the thread, bring the needle up just inside the marked turning line of an appliqué shape. Start away from a point or deep inner curve.

2. Use the tip of a wooden toothpick to turn under the fabric, so that the turning line is just out of sight. The rough surface of the wood will grab the seam allowance, giving you better control over the fabric. When you're happy with the way the fabric looks, lightly crease the fold with your left thumbnail, creating a crisp, easy-to-stitch edge about ¼" long.

3. For the first stitch, pull the thread out at a right angle to the fold. Insert the tip of the needle into the background fabric, right next to the point where the thread exits the appliqué shape.

4. Bring the needle up through the background fabric a short distance to the left, just catching the edge of the appliqué shape. Catch only 1 or 2 threads of the fold. This step determines your stitch length, which, in my experience, is different for almost everyone. I enjoy making tiny stitches (20 to 24 or more per inch) because they allow me to stitch smoother curves and sharper points. Try taking tiny stitches, especially in sticky situations such as steep outer points and deep inner curves. Determine the stitch length you prefer, and stick with whatever length feels comfortable and gives you results you like.

5. Bring the needle all the way through the fabric, and pull the thread out at a right angle again to determine where to insert the needle for your next stitch. Continue stitching, keeping the intervals between stitches even.

6. To end a thread, insert the needle into the background fabric as though you were going to take another stitch, but bring it through to the wrong side. Wind the thread around the needle twice, and insert the tip of the needle between the background fabric and the fabric of the appliqué shape underneath.

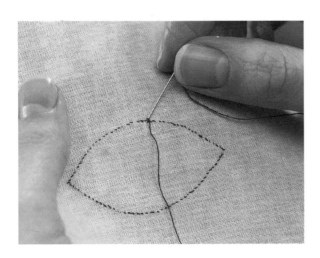

7. Pull the thread all the way out of the background fabric, leaving a small French knot on the surface. Tug on the thread to pop the knot out of sight. Clip the thread close to the fabric.

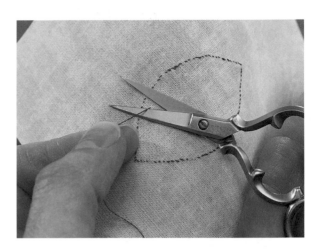

Finishing

ALL of the blocks in this book use the same finishing techniques. After you finish stitching, think about whether you want to hand quilt inside any of the appliqué shapes. If you do, trim away the background fabric underneath those areas, leaving $3/16$" to $1/4$" seam allowances. Take care to separate the fabric layers carefully, and use a sharp pair of embroidery scissors.

To give your appliqué a crisp finish, spray the wrong side of your work very lightly with spray sizing, and press it with a hot, dry iron set on "cotton." Spray the front side of your block with spray sizing; then press it again. Place the block on a rotary-cutting mat, and center a $9\frac{1}{2}$"-square quilter's ruler over your work. Use a rotary cutter to trim the finished block to $9\frac{1}{2}$" square.

Gallery of Quilts

*E*ACH OF THE QUILTS shown in this section was made by a quiltmaker who participated in a sixteen-month-long series of classes I taught at the Summer House Needleworks Shop in Oley, Pennsylvania. In our first artful appliqué class, we talked about how bright colors can make a flower stand out visually and discussed effective ways to surround flowers with leaves in darker, dustier hues.

From that point on, each student began to think about how she personally wanted to combine colors, focusing on including lots of different values and fabric types. The goal was only to achieve results that pleased each person's innate preferences. With the passing months, each quilter developed a unique color palette and sense of creativity. As you browse through the photos on the following pages, I think you'll agree that the results are spectacular.

LEARNING TO FLY

44" x 44"

Jane's techniques and tips have given me a new freedom in approaching appliqué; it's like learning to fly!
—Joan Settle Thomas, 1999, Montgomery County, Pennsylvania

SECOND SATURDAY OF THE MONTH

50" x 63"

This quilt delightfully consumed my life for seventeen months, and its name came from the day of the month that our class met. Because of this class, I now eat, sleep, and dream appliqué and have a hard time sitting down without a needle and thread in my hand. I also acquired new tastes in color, since I had always been a pastels person. Now I have the confidence to tackle any appliqué project that may come my way.

—Ellen M. Voguit, 1999, St. Augustine, Florida

SATURDAY MORNING FRIENDSHIP GARDEN
56" x 56"

What started out as a one-day trip to take an appliqué class with Jane turned out to be a sixteen-month adventure for me and my friends Debbie and Rosemarie. Every second Saturday of the month, we'd leave New Jersey at 7:00 A.M. for the two-hour trip to Pennsylvania, eagerly awaiting the new techniques we'd be shown. With all the wonderful tricks Jane showed us, my appliqué skills were sharpened to a new level. I love color, any color, so these blocks were an opportunity to play and explore.
—Rhonda Kleiman, 1999, Fords, New Jersey

METAMORPHOSIS

57" x 57"

This quilt has completely changed the way I look at colors and fabrics. When I saw Jane's and the other students' blocks, I was inspired to experiment with bright and wild fabrics. This quilt will really shock other quilters I know, because they would never expect me to go this wild. I feel I have learned to spread my wings and soar with colors.

—Deborah A. Gardner, 1999, Colonia, New Jersey

WEEKENDS IN OLEY VALLEY
58" x 58"

*It's easy to spend a weekend in rural Pennsylvania at a quilt store with Jane and other avid appliquérs.
Jane always brought a new or easier approach to a project. As I worked on the Winter Cardinal block (in the
upper right corner), I couldn't believe how easily it went together. Jane's cutwork appliqué technique made it easy
to stitch the vine, and I used the technique again to stitch the taupe and blue fabrics in the outer border.*
—Grace I. Sohn, 1999, Essex, Connecticut

BIRD IN THE WINDOW

31" x 31"

I combined parts of three different lessons to make this wall hanging, which was machine quilted by
Carol Heisler. My favorite technique is using a hera marker to score the fabric.
It makes such a nice, crisp line for turning under a seam allowance.
—Dorothy W. Murdoch, 1999, West Chester, Pennsylvania

Always in Hand
38" x 48"

Jane's class has made me addicted to the art of appliqué. The techniques she taught made stitching fun. I called my quilt "Always in Hand" because I took my sewing bag, which contained my blocks-in-progress, everywhere I went. That's why I like appliqué so much—you can take it with you almost anywhere and it is very rewarding.

—Mary L. Bagenstose, 1999, Womelsdorf, Pennsylvania

SPLIT PERSONALITY
54" x 75"

I started Jane's class as an excuse to make a monthly trip to my favorite quilt shop, Summer House Needleworks. My quilt is called "Split Personality" because, although the blocks were hand appliquéd, I couldn't resist adding machine work. I found that appliqué is extremely relaxing, and I was eager to work on it every night. I also discovered that my "alter ego" had different color preferences. One side of me loved neutral tones, while the other side loved bright, vibrant colors. —Rosemarie DeSalvo, 1999, Linden, New Jersey

JANE AND ME
24" x 44"

Jane was the inspiration behind my first attempt at appliqué and hand quilting. I combined several of my favorite blocks in an asymmetrical design linked by my own variation of Jane's Irish Spring block. Making all the blocks in Jane's class has expanded my appreciation of and fascination with the infinite diversity of color and fabric. This small quilt will be a cedar-chest cover.
—Diana Lynn Channer, 1999, Schwenksville, Pennsylvania

ROSE'S GARDEN

63" x 74"

Although I started quilting in 1978, Jane's was my first quilting class, and I loved it. I started this quilt on January 20, 1999, and finished it on August 21, 1999. —Rose King, 1999, Wyomissing, Pennsylvania

YES, JANE—NOT ALL LEAVES ARE GREEN,
BUT SOME ARE GREENER THAN OTHERS!

25" x 23"

*My love of appliqué came about when I started commuting to Manhattan. I needed something portable
that I could do on the train or bus, and appliqué was it. Taking classes with Jane brought my appliqué to the next
level, thanks to her wonderful techniques and tips. My friends say my greatest quilting accomplishment
is the ability to thread a #11 Straw needle in any moving vehicle—train, car, or bus.*
—*Joan Flanigan-Clarke, 1999, Mahwah, New Jersey*

CONFIDENT BEGINNER IN PARADISE
16" x 16"

Little did I know that when I drove 110 miles to a quilt shop in Pennsylvania in the summer of 1998, it would change my quilt life—from piecing to appliqué. After exploring the books and fabrics, I found the classroom where Jane was conducting an appliqué class. The samples were the most beautiful blocks I had ever seen. I joined the class at block five, and this pillow was made from the second appliqué block I made. I'm proud of the accomplishment. A beginner to appliqué, my classmates were constantly encouraging me, even when they finished well ahead of me. The class also allowed me to spend a few hours in a quilter's paradise.
—Gayle Lynn Rosenbach, 1999, Springfield, New Jersey

Appliqué Blocks

*I*NSPIRATION FOR APPLIQUÉ designs can come from almost anywhere—flowers, foliage, trees, animals, architecture, or something as simple as a decorative object you have in your home. Accompanying each block is a description of what inspired me to create it: a snowy winter landscape in Nebraska, rich terracotta tones in buildings around Phoenix, stars shining in the night sky, a motif from an antique quilt, even a classic patchwork pattern.

Choose a block you like and browse through the quilts on pages 21–33 to see how many different looks you can find for that design. You'll soon realize that these blocks look great in any color palette; there are no right or wrong color combinations, and no color rules to follow. Enjoy the fun of making a quilt in the colors your heart desires.

Choosing a Design

THESE SIXTEEN BLOCKS are presented in the same order that the instructions appear in this book. The designs feature a progression of techniques, ranging from simple buds in the first block to a complex, multipetal tulip unit in the last. The instructions for each block start with a list of techniques used. Read through these to get a feel for the demands and learning opportunities presented by individual blocks. If you are new to hand appliqué, start with the first block, and then move on to others that feature techniques interesting to you.

Vintage Flower and Buds
Page 38

Windblown Tulip
Page 44

Scalloped Leaf Wheel
Page 50

Winter Cardinal
Page 56

Cactus Flower
Page 62

Cotton-Boll Blossom
Page 68

Flight of Fancy
Page 74

Square Wreath
Page 80

Summer Nosegay
Page 86

Dove and Dogwood Blossoms
Page 94

Delicate Dahlia
Page 100

Irish Spring
Page 108

Dresden Flower
Page 114

Hummingbird and Trillium
Page 120

Starshine
Page 128

Twining Lily
Page 134

*T*HIS LITTLE TULIP *is similar to many I've seen in nineteenth-century appliqué quilts. It's a great starting point for learning hand appliqué because it contains almost every shape you might ever need to stitch—gentle inner and outer curves, deep inner curves, sharp inner and outer points, and very narrow shapes.*

TECHNIQUES

- ⚭ Cutwork appliqué (stems)
- ⚭ Unit appliqué (buds)
- ⚭ Modified cutwork appliqué (flower)
- ⚭ Open seam allowances (buds and flower)

FABRICS

- ⚭ 11" square for background
- ⚭ 11" square for stems
- ⚭ 5" square for flower
- ⚭ Two 2" squares for buds
- ⚭ 12 assorted 2" squares for leaves

STITCHING THE CUTWORK STEM

1. Mark the center of the block background by folding the square in half twice and finger-pressing the folds at the center. Trace the stem pattern (page 43) onto freezer paper, making sure to mark the crossed lines that indicate the block center. Cut out the template and press it onto the stem fabric. Mark around the template. Remove the freezer paper and layer the marked square of stem fabric over the background square, matching the centers. Pin the layers together at the center and corners.

2. Working from the upper left side of the straight stem and cutting only into the stem fabric, cut a 3/16" seam al-lowance along the stem for about 1½". Bring a needle up from underneath the stem fabric, just inside the marked turning line at the top of the stem. Use a wooden toothpick to turn under the seam allowance on the marked line for about ½". Crease the turned edge gently with your thumbnail, and appliqué as far as you cut. Continue cutting and appliquéing in 1½" to 2" segments until you approach the inner point where the stem changes direction.

3. Clip the seam allowance up to the marked inner point, and then cut a seam allowance along the next edge of the stem. Make several clips, ¼" apart, in the curved seam allowance. Stitch the curved edge, ending your stitching 1" *before* you reach the calyx. Cut a seam allowance around the calyx and along the other side of the stem. Appliqué the second edge of the stem, starting your stitches directly across from the previous stitching. Letting the calyx hang free makes it easy to stitch to the bud fabric later.

Stitch around the remainder of the stem in the same manner. Do not turn under and stitch the upper edge of the stem, because the flower will overlap it.

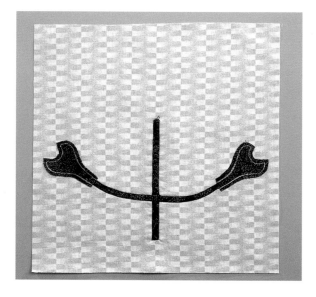

To CONTROL STRAY *threads that sometimes pop out at inner points, run the tip of a toothpick over a water-soluble gluestick. Insert the toothpick under the inner point, tucking in any exposed threads. Pinch the fabric slightly to make sure the threads stay out of sight. Take one stitch to reinforce the inner point, and continue stitching.*

STITCHING THE BUD

1. Make several short clips along the inner curved edge of 1 calyx, stopping just short of the marked turning line. Pin the calyx to a small square of bud fabric and appliqué the inner curve. Trace and cut out a freezer-paper bud template; then press it next to the stitched inner curve. Mark around the upper edge of the bud template, as shown.

2. Cut a 3/16" seam allowance around the bud, and trim the bud fabric even with the seam allowance of the calyx underneath. On the wrong side of the bud unit, make 2 small clips into the seam allowance, ½" from the edges. Finger-press these portions of the seam allowances open, as shown. The opened seam allowances will lie flat and be easy to turn under, allowing you to create a smooth join where the bud and the calyx meet.

3. Stitch the other bud unit together as you did the first. Referring to the block photo (page 38), stitch both bud units to the background square. Change thread colors as necessary to completely stitch the bud units.

STITCHING THE FLOWER: CONQUERING CURVES AND POINTS

1. Trace the flower pattern (page 43) onto freezer paper. Cut out the template and press it onto the flower fabric. Mark around the template. Remove the freezer paper, and cut a 3/16" seam allowance around the flower, *except* where there are deep curves, as shown. This modified form of cutwork will keep the narrow parts of the flower properly positioned, because you won't cut the seam allowances around the deep curves until you're ready to stitch them.

2. Appliqué the flower over the top edge of the stem. When you reach the untrimmed, deep inner curves, cut and stitch only a short distance at a time.

At the deepest part of an inner curve, keep your seam allowance as narrow as you feel comfortable with. Make several short clips about ⅛" apart into the seam allowance.

ALL LEAVES ARE NOT ALIKE

1. Although all the leaves in the block (page 38) started with the same template, it's easy to see that the stitched leaves aren't identical. This comes from letting a toothpick and needle shape the leaves as you stitch. Trace one of the leaf patterns you like (page 43) onto template plastic and cut it out, adding a ³⁄₁₆" seam allowance. Mark and cut out 12 leaves in a variety of colors.

When you're not sure what colors you really like together, try dumping your scrap bag or a selection of fabrics from your stash onto a table and leave the fabrics out for a day or two. Every once in a while, walk by and scramble them up a bit. Then stand back to see if something interesting jumps out at you visually.

2. Referring to the block photo (page 38) for placement, pin 12 leaves along the stems in pairs. Appliqué them so that the points touch the same spots on opposite sides of the stems. Placing the leaves directly opposite each other makes them look "right" to a viewer. Don't worry about making the spaces even *between* leaf pairs. The eye will not notice small differences, and your leaves will have a natural appearance.

Try cutting out a variety of leaves in many different colors. Experiment with various color combinations, and save the leaves you don't use—they're bound to come in handy for future blocks!

*Y*OU CAN ALMOST *see the leaves on this little tulip dancing merrily in a breeze. I chose different values of a single color for the flower, and subtle variations of another color for the upper and lower layers of the layered leaves. Try my approach, or combine several different shades for the leaves.*

TECHNIQUES

- Cutwork appliqué (stem)
- Reverse appliqué (leaves)
- Stitching beyond marked shapes (tulip)
- Open seam allowances (tulip)
- Unit appliqué (tulip)
- Modified cutwork appliqué (bird)

FABRICS

- 11" square for background
- 6" square for stem
- 5" square for side tulip petals
- 5" square for middle tulip petal
- 7 assorted 3" squares for lower layers of leaves
- 7 assorted 3" squares for upper layers of leaves
- 4" square for bird

STITCHING THE CUTWORK STEM

1. Mark the center of the block background by folding the square in half twice and finger-pressing the folds at the center. Trace the stem pattern (page 49) onto freezer paper, making sure to mark the crossed lines that indicate the block center. Cut out the template, making sure to cut *around* the block-center marking to leave it intact. Press the template onto the stem fabric, matching the centers. Mark around the template, except where the block center is marked. Remove the freezer paper. Join the lines of the stem if you like. Layer the marked stem fabric over the background square, matching the centers, and pin at the center and corners.

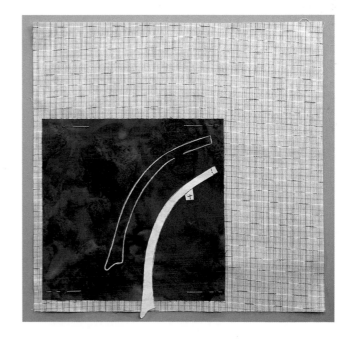

2. Cut a ³/₁₆" seam allowance along the stem for about 1½". Appliqué as far as you cut; then continue cutting and appliquéing 1½" segments until the stem is completely stitched.

ADDING THE LAYERED Leaves

1. Trace one of the leaf patterns (page 49) onto template plastic, marking both "windows." Cut out the template and mark around it on your upper-layer leaf fabric. Mark 7 leaf tops.

2. Cut a ³/₁₆" seam allowance inside 1 window area. Do *not* cut a seam allowance around the outside of the leaf yet—the extra fabric will make it easier to stitch the window areas. Make several short clips into the seam allowance around the inner curves and at the corners, spacing your clips ⅛" apart. Pin the marked leaf onto a square of fabric for the lower layer. Starting in the middle of the straight edge, reverse-appliqué the window shape. Repeat to appliqué the second window shape.

3. Make 7 layered leaves, varying the colors of the underlying layers. After both window areas are stitched, cut a ³/₁₆" seam allowance around the outer edges of the leaf top. Trim the lower fabric layer even with the seam allowances of the window shapes.

*F*OR VARIETY, *use 2 different fabrics for the window shapes in some leaves. After completing the first window shape, stitch the next one onto a different solid or print fabric.*

4. Referring to the block photo (page 44), stitch the layered leaves to the background square, spacing them evenly along the stem. On the left side, notice that the second leaf from the top does *not* have a partner across from it.

STITCHING THE TULIP UNIT

1. Trace the tulip pattern (page 49) onto freezer paper, keeping the shapes joined to ensure that your finished tulip will fit together accurately. Where the side petals meet the middle petal, mark short hatch marks and label the outer petals "left" and "right". Cut the template apart to make 3 templates. Press the *left* and *right* petal templates onto the side-petal fabric. Mark around the templates, marking the hatch marks in the seam allowances, as shown.

2. Cut a ³/₁₆" seam allowance around each petal, and clip the seam allowances at the hatch marks. Stitch the right petal to the middle-petal fabric, starting at the hatch mark. Do not stitch the upper portion of the right petal. When you reach the bottom of the petal, take a few stitches *beyond* the end of the petal, as shown. Stitching beyond the petal will help you turn under a smooth edge when you appliqué the completed tulip unit to the background square.

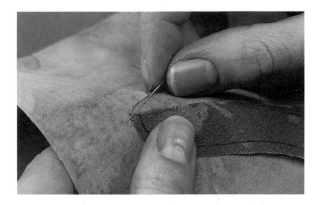

3. Press the middle-petal template next to the stitched right petal. Mark around the top of the template, then remove the freezer paper. Stitch the left petal to the middle-petal fabric so that it meets the right petal at the bottom, as shown. Make sure the clipped seam allowance matches the left edge of the marked middle petal.

4. Cut a ³/₁₆" seam allowance around the middle petal, trimming the fabric underneath even with the seam allowances. On the wrong side of the tulip unit, make a clip into the seam allowance on each side of the middle petal, ¼" from the upper edge. Finger-press these portions of the seam allowances open, as shown, so that they lie flat. The open seam allowances will enable you to stitch smooth joins between the shapes.

5. Referring to the block photo (page 44) for placement, stitch the tulip unit to the background fabric, changing thread colors as needed.

STITCHING THE BIRD

1. Trace the bird pattern (page 49) onto freezer paper, and cut it out. Press the template onto the bird fabric. Mark around the template and remove the freezer paper. Cut out the bird shape, leaving a ³/₁₆" seam allowance except at areas with deep curves.

2. Referring to the block photo below for placement, stitch the bird to the background near the stem and leaves. In the deep inner curves of the wings, cut and stitch only a small distance at a time.

JUST FOR FUN, *appliqué the bird with its beak next to a leaf so that it looks as though the bird is nibbling.*

Scalloped Leaf Wheel

*A*T FIRST GLANCE, *this Scalloped Leaf Wheel design seems symmetrical. A second look reveals that the flower has seven petals. There are twenty scallops around the circle and sixteen leaves around the scallops. The asymmetrical quality creates a whimsical folk-art feel.*

TECHNIQUES

- ⚘ Unit appliqué (scalloped center and leaves)
- ⚘ Modified cutwork appliqué (flower)
- ⚘ Scored turning lines (circle)
- ⚘ Broderie-perse appliqué (circle)
- ⚘ Open seam allowances (leaves)

FABRICS

- ⚘ 11" square for background
- ⚘ 4" square for flower
- ⚘ Small scrap for center circle
- ⚘ 7" square for scalloped circle
- ⚘ 7" square for wheel-center background
- ⚘ Two 2" squares for each leaf unit (32 squares total)

STITCHING THE CENTER UNIT

1. Trace the scalloped circle shape (page 55) onto freezer paper, marking the inner circle and the outer scalloped edge. Cut out the template; then press it onto the scalloped-circle fabric and mark around both the inner and outer edges. Remove the freezer paper and pin the marked shape to the wheel-center background fabric. Use cutwork appliqué to stitch the inner edge of the circle. Trim the fabric around the scalloped edge, leaving a $3/16$" seam allowance. Trim the wheel-center background fabric underneath to a $3/16$" seam allowance, as shown.

*A*FTER TRIMMING THE *scalloped edges, press the unit flat with a hot, dry iron set on "cotton." Pressing the unit makes it easier to add the flower and small center circle that come next.*

2. Trace the flower pattern (page 55) onto freezer paper, and cut it out. Press the template onto the flower fabric and mark around the edges. Remove the freezer paper and cut a 3/16" seam allowance around the outer edges of the flower, leaving the fabric between the petals uncut. Pin the marked flower to the stitched center unit, matching centers. Stitch, cutting the seam allowances in the deeply curved areas only as you reach them, as shown.

Use a colorful batik for the flower in this block. These closely woven fabrics tend to fray less than standard quilting cottons, which allows you to cut narrower seam allowances. Using very narrow seam allowances makes it easier to stitch beautiful inner and outer curves on the petals.

3. Referring to the block photo (page 50) for placement, appliqué the scalloped edges of the center unit to the background square.

ADDING THE CENTER CIRCLE

1. You can create the small center circle in 2 different ways. One method is to use a broderie-perse technique. Choose a printed fabric with interesting circle designs. Cut out a circle, leaving a 3/16" seam allowance, and appliqué it to the center of the flower. This technique may change the way you look at fabric—you'll start seeing circle designs everywhere you shop.

Another method is to score a circle with any round, cylindrical object that has a sharp edge, such as a clean, metal lipstick-tube top. Place a small piece of fabric on a padded surface, wrong side up. Press hard on the lipstick tube with the palm of your hand and twist it without changing its position on the fabric. This will produce an easy-to-see, scored circle on the fabric. The more pressure you apply, the easier it will be to see the scored circle.

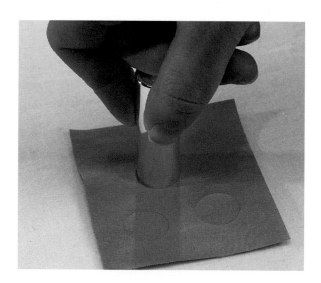

2. Cut a 3/16" seam allowance around the scored circle, and stitch the circle to the center of the flower.

*T*RY A VARIATION *on this Scalloped Leaf Wheel design by substituting a different shape for the 7-petaled flower. Consider using the dogwood blossom from Dove and Dogwood Blossoms block (page 94) or a bird from one of the other designs. If a shape is too large or small, reduce or enlarge it with a photocopy machine.*

STITCHING THE LEAVES

1. Trace a leaf (page 55) onto template plastic, and cut it out. Fold a 2" square of leaf fabric in half diagonally, wrong sides together, and crease the fold. Pin the folded square onto an unfolded square of leaf fabric, matching the edges. Stitch the fold from beginning to end. Trim the folded fabric underneath, leaving a 3/16" seam allowance. Finger-press the seam allowance open.

   Working from the right side of the fabric, place the leaf template over the stitched square. Align the ends of the leaf with the seam, and mark around the template, as shown. Cut a 3/16" seam allowance around the leaf. Repeat this process to make 16 two-part leaf units.

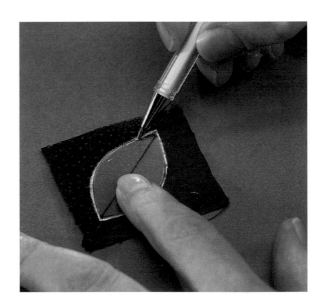

2. Lightly finger-press a diagonal fold in both directions on the background square. Pin a leaf on each of the folds, just outside the scalloped circle. Pin a leaf unit at the top, bottom, and sides of the block; then pin and stitch a leaf in each of the remaining spaces—just eyeball the placement.

DURING A 1997 Christmas visit with family, I noticed the twirling wings of a cardinal in one of my mother's favorite holiday mobiles. I sketched its curves on a scrap of paper, and the result was the fanciful bird in this block. A snowy Nebraska landscape with empty tree branches contributed to my choice of light and dark prints for the backgrounds and the winding black vine that separates them in this design.

TECHNIQUES

- Cutwork appliqué (vine)
- Unit appliqué (cardinal and two-part background)
- Open seam allowances (cardinal)
- Choosing a focal-point color (leaves)
- Balancing color values (leaves)

FABRICS

- 11" light-value square for lower-right background
- 11" medium-value square for upper-left background
- 11" dark-value square for vine
- 5" square for cardinal's body
- Small scrap for beak
- 18 assorted 2" squares for leaves

STITCHING THE CUTWORK VINE

1. Trace the vine pattern (page 61) onto freezer paper, extending the lines of the vine evenly on both sides until they are long enough to match the 11" background square. Cut out the template and press it onto the dark fabric. Mark along the inner and outer edges of the vine.

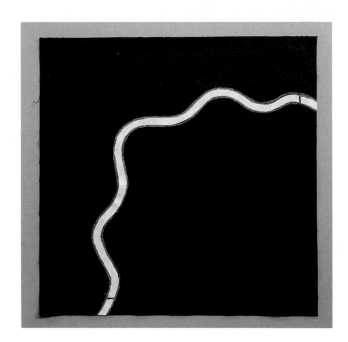

2. Remove the freezer paper and pin the marked vine fabric onto the light-value background fabric, aligning the edges. Beginning at the lower end of the marked vine, cut a 3/16" seam allowance along the inner edge for about 2", cutting only through the dark fabric. Appliqué as far as you cut; then stop.

3. Cut and stitch another 2" portion of seam allowance. Continue stitching in segments until the inner edge of the vine is completely stitched, as shown. Trim the light-value fabric underneath, leaving a 3/16" seam allowance.

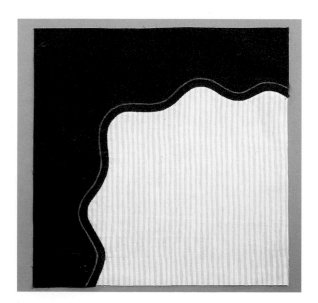

4. Pin the half-stitched vine square onto the medium-value fabric, aligning the edges. Stitch the other edge of the vine, as shown. Trim the medium fabric underneath, leaving a 3/16" seam al-lowance. Press the completed background square with a hot, dry iron set to "cotton."

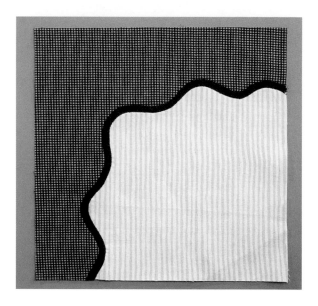

STITCHING THE CARDINAL

1. Trace the joined cardinal and beak (page 61), onto freezer paper. Cut the templates apart. Press the template for the cardinal's body onto the cardinal fabric and mark around it, as shown. Remove the freezer paper, but do *not* cut out the bird at this time.

2. Press the beak template onto the beak fabric and mark around it. Remove the freezer paper and cut out the beak shape, adding a ¼" seam allowance (notice that this is wider than usual). Stitch the beak to the cardinal's head, beginning and ending your stitching beyond the marked cardinal's head. This will join the beak and cardinal's head securely and make it easy to stitch the bird to the background fabric without any gaps between the 2 shapes.

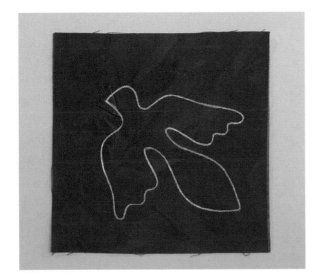

*T*RY USING A *fun print for the cardinal in this block. Look for colorful fabrics that feature strong curves or swirls that could simulate the look of feathers.*

3. Cut a 3/16" seam allowance around the cardinal, including the beak as well. On the wrong side, finger-press the seam allowance between the beak and the cardinal's head open to distribute the fabric evenly on both sides of the seam.

4. Pin and stitch the cardinal unit to the middle of the light background area, as shown.

ADDING THE LEAVES

1. With a permanent pen, trace one of the leaf patterns (page 61) onto template plastic, and cut it out.

2. Mark and cut 18 leaves from the assorted leaf fabrics. Refer to "Choosing Leaf Colors" below. Pin the leaves in place; then appliqué.

To CHECK COLOR VALUES, *use a photographer's tool called a Wratten filter. This small, amber-colored square of Plexiglas shows the relative lightness and darkness of any color. Look for this product at a camera shop.*

Choosing Leaf Colors

- *When I teach this block in class, I suggest that students use a color that's lighter or brighter than the others for the leaf at the upper-left corner. Because light and bright colors tend to advance visually, this helps lead the viewer's eye upward, enhancing the feeling of a cardinal in flight.*

- *Balancing the values (the relative lightness and darkness) of the leaf colors is the key to success. Count how many different colors you see in the block photo (page 56). Some leaf colors are warm, such as the rust one, while others are cool, such as the turquoise leaf in the upper-left corner. Whatever colors you choose, place the color* values *evenly on both sides of the vine. For example, if you place a dark magenta leaf at an outer edge of the vine, balance it with another dark leaf in a different color at the opposite edge. Follow this principle whether your values are light, medium, or dark, and refer to the block photo for guidance.*

Arrows indicate where
to lengthen vine template
for an 11" square of fabric.

Lower edge of block

Cactus Flower

*T*HE COLORS IN *this block remind me of the brilliant red, purple, and terra-cotta tones in architecture around Phoenix, Arizona. Vibrant desert blossoms in that region inspired the flowers, giving this block an overall effect that is light, airy, and fun.*

TECHNIQUES

- Making 1 template from multiple shapes (cactus flower and vase)
- Cutwork appliqué (stems and calyx)
- Stitching beyond marked shapes (vase)
- Open seam allowances (vase and flower)
- Reverse appliqué (heart)
- Echoing colors (flowers and leaves)

FABRICS

- 11" square for background
- 3" square for center flower petal
- 4" x 5" piece for inner flower petals
- 4" x 7" piece for outer flower petals
- 7" square for stems and calyx
- 5" square for body of vase
- 3" x 5" piece for rickrack stripe
- 3" square for heart
- 5" square for base of vase
- 10 assorted 2" squares for leaves

STITCHING THE CUTWORK STEMS

1. Mark the center of the block background by folding the square in half twice and finger-pressing the folds at the center. Trace the stems and calyx (page 67) onto freezer paper, joining them at the bottom to create a single template. Joining the pieces makes it easy to position the vase over the stems later. Mark the crossed lines that indicate the block center on the middle stem, and cut out the template. Press it onto the stem fabric and mark around it; include the block center mark. Remove the freezer paper and pin the marked stem fabric onto the background square, matching the centers.

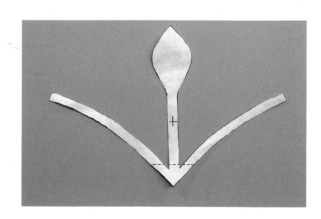

2. Stitch the stems, starting with the left stem and working your way up to 1" from the calyx. End the stitching at this point, and clip the seam allowance. Cut a ³/₁₆" seam allowance around the calyx, and make another clip in the seam allowance across from the previous clip. Stitch the remaining portion of the stem. Allowing the calyx to hang free, as shown, makes it easier to stitch the calyx to the flower unit later.

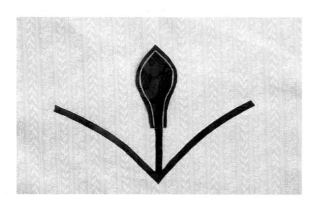

STITCHING THE FLOWER

1. Trace the center flower petal (page 67) onto freezer paper, extending the lines in the lower portion to form a leaf shape. Include small hatch marks to indicate where to stitch the petal to the next layer of fabric. Cut out the template and press it onto the center-petal fabric. Mark around the template, and mark the hatch marks in the seam allowance. Remove the freezer paper and cut a ³/₁₆" seam allowance around the petal.

2. Pin the petal onto a piece of inner-petal fabric. Note that nothing is marked on the inner-petal fabric yet. Clip the seam allowance of the center petal at the hatch marks, and stitch the lower part of the petal to the inner-petal fabric, beginning at one clip and ending at the other.

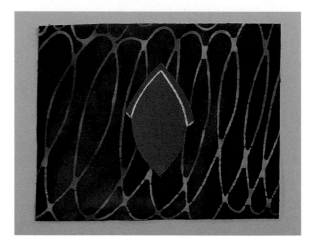

3. Trace the 2 inner petals (page 67) onto freezer paper, connecting the petals and outlining the lower part of the center petal with dotted lines to make 1 template from 2 shapes. Mark hatch marks at the outer edges where these inner petals will meet the outer petals. Cut out the template and press it onto the partially stitched flower unit, aligning it with the center petal. Mark around the edges of the inner petals, extending the hatch marks into the seam allowances, as shown.

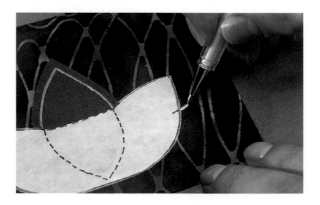

4. Remove the freezer paper and cut a 3/16" seam allowance around the inner petals. Trim the inner-petal fabric underneath the center petal, leaving a 3/16" seam allowance. Make clips into the seam allowances at the hatch marks on each side of the inner petals. Stitch the inner petals to a piece of outer-petal fabric, beginning at one clip and ending at the other, as shown. Trace the outer petals (page 67) onto freezer paper, connecting them as before. Cut out the template and press it onto the partially stitched flower unit. Mark around the outer petals and remove the freezer paper; then cut them out, leaving a 3/16" seam allowance.

5. Referring to the photo (page 62) for placement, pin the calyx over the flower unit. Stitch, beginning and ending the stitching inside the marked lines of the outer petals. Stitch the calyx-and-flower unit to the background square, changing thread colors as needed.

JOINING THE VASE UNIT

1. Trace the vase (page 67) onto freezer paper, including the heart and rickrack stripe. Make hatch marks where the bottom of the vase touches the base. Cut the templates apart.

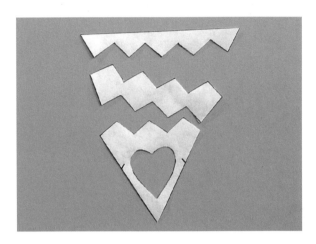

2. Press the rickrack template onto the appropriate fabric and mark around it. Remove the freezer paper and cut around the rickrack, leaving a 3/16" seam allowance except at the sides, which should have 1/4" seam allowances. Stitch the top and bottom edges of the rickrack to the

vase-body fabric, as shown, beginning and ending about ⅛" beyond the vase's side edge. Press the top and bottom vase-body templates next to the rickrack, and mark around them to complete the main part of the vase. Before removing the freezer paper, mark hatch marks in the seam allowances to indicate where to stitch the vase to the base fabric.

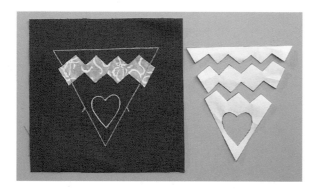

3. Cut a ³/₁₆" seam allowance inside the marked heart shape. Layer the heart fabric underneath the vase fabric and reverse appliqué the heart, as shown. On the wrong side of the block, trim the fabric, leaving a ³/₁₆" seam allowance around the heart.

4. On each side of the vase, make clips into the seam allowance at the hatch marks. Stitch the lower portion of the vase to the base fabric, starting at one clip and ending at the other, as

shown. Trace the base pattern (page 67) onto freezer paper, connecting the triangular shapes with dashed lines. Press the template onto the vase unit, and mark around the edges. Remove the freezer paper and cut a ³/₁₆" seam allowance around the base to complete the vase unit.

5. Trim the vase fabric underneath the rickrack stripe, leaving a ³/₁₆" seam allowance. Clip into the seam allowances about ¼" from each edge, and finger-press these short segments open. Pressing open the seam allowances lets the piece lie flat, making it easier to stitch the vase unit to the background square.

6. Referring to the block photo (page 62) for placement, stitch the vase unit to the background square so that it overlaps the lower edges of the stems.

Adding the Leaves

1. With a permanent marker, trace one of the leaf patterns (page 67) onto template plastic, and cut it out.

2. Mark and cut 10 leaves from the assorted leaf fabrics. Pin the leaves in place; then appliqué. Choose leaf fabrics that echo the colors in the flower unit. Balance the colors by placing similar values in the same positions on opposite stems.

Cotton-Boll Blossom

*T*HIS DESIGN CAME *from doing some impromptu doodles during a long telephone call. While my left brain was occupied with listening and speaking, my right brain was free to produce squiggles, curves, lines, and interesting shapes. Keep a pencil and paper by your telephone, and try sketching while you talk—you may create a gorgeous, original quilt design.*

TECHNIQUES

- ☙ Modified cutwork appliqué (stem and underlying stamens)
- ☙ Making 1 template from multiple shapes (stamens)
- ☙ Unit appliqué (cotton-boll blossom)
- ☙ Using a window template (cotton-boll blossom)
- ☙ Stitching beyond marked shapes (leaves)
- ☙ Color outlines (leaves)

FABRICS

- ☙ 11" square for background
- ☙ 8" square for stem and overlying stamens
- ☙ 5" square for underlying stamens
- ☙ 5" square for cotton-boll blossom
- ☙ 7 assorted 3" squares for leaves
- ☙ Two 3" squares of silk douppioni or cotton for leaf outlines
- ☙ 4" square for bird

PREPARING THE CUTWORK STEM

1. Trace the stem and overlying stamens (page 73) onto freezer paper, and cut out the template. Press the template onto the stem fabric and mark around it.

2. Remove the freezer paper. Roughly cut a ¾" seam allowance around the lower part of the stem. The wide seam allowance will keep the stem from stretching out of shape, prevent frayed seam allowances, and make it easy to position the stem accurately on the background fabric. Cut a ³/₁₆" seam allowance around the upper portion of the stem and each of the stamens, as shown.

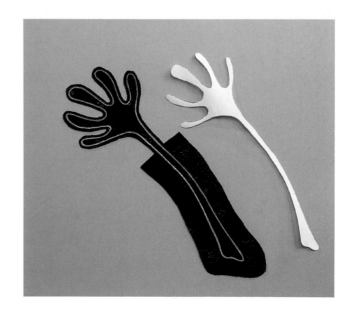

STITCHING THE
COTTON-BOLL BLOSSOM

1. Trace the underlying stamens shape (page 73) onto freezer paper, and cut out the template. Press it onto the underlying-stamen fabric and mark around it. Remove the freezer paper and cut a 3/16" seam allowance around the stamens, but do not cut between them. Stitch the underlying stamens to the cotton-boll blossom fabric, cutting the seam allowances between the stamens only when you reach them.

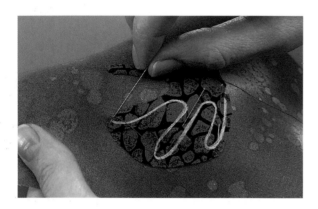

To CREATE A BLENDED *look in the different pieces of the cotton-boll blossom, choose colors that are similar in value (lightness or darkness). To make the flower or the underlying stamens stand out from the rest of the blossom, use* different *values.*

2. Stitch the overlying stamens over the underlying stamens. Stitch each overlying stamen only to within ¼" of the upper curved edge. Keeping the tops of the stamens free makes it easier to stitch them to the background square later. If necessary, adjust the placements to keep the spaces between the stamens even.

   Make a window template by tracing the outline of the cotton-boll blossom (page 73) onto freezer paper. Roughly cut a square around the shape; then cut on the drawn lines to form a window template. Place the template over the stitched stamens. Mark inside the lines, making slight adjustments to the curves between stamens if necessary. Remove the freezer paper, as shown.

3. Without cutting through the lower portion of the stem, cut a 3/16" seam allowance around the cotton-boll blossom. Referring to the block photo (page 68) for placement, stitch the blossom unit to the background square, changing thread colors as necessary.

ADDING THE LEAVES

1. Outlining a leaf with a hint of different color is a subtle way to lend unity to a color scheme. Trace the main portion of an outlined leaf (page 73) onto template plastic, and cut it out. Mark a little X on this template to indicate which edge to stitch to the second fabric. Mark around the template on a piece of leaf fabric. Cut out the leaf, leaving a 3/16" seam allowance.

   If using silk douppioni, apply a soft, sheer tricot interfacing to the wrong side to add body and avoid frayed edges during appliqué.

2. Stitch the marked leaf edge to the second fabric, beginning and ending the stitching just beyond the marked leaf points.

3. Mark a slight curve from point to point on the "outline" fabric—you can eyeball this. Start at one point and end at the other.

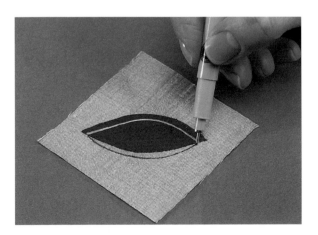

4. Cut a 3/16" seam allowance around the leaf, and trim the fabric underneath as well, leaving a 3/16" seam allowance. On the wrong side of the leaf, clip into the seam allowance 1/4" from each point. Finger-press the short seam-allowance segments open.

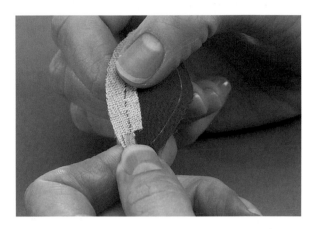

5. Make another outlined leaf, turning the template over so that the outlined edge lies in the opposite direction.

6. Trace a full-leaf pattern (page 73) onto template plastic and cut it out. Mark around the template on 5 squares of leaf fabric. Cut out the leaves, leaving a 3/16" seam allowance. Referring to the block photo for placement, stitch all of the leaves next to the stem.

STITCHING THE BIRD

1. Trace the bird pattern (page 73) onto freezer paper and cut it out. Press this template onto the bird fabric and mark around it. Remove the freezer paper.

2. Pin the bird to the background fabric and stitch it in place.

*W*HENEVER YOU FIND *a block design you enjoy stitching, look for creative ways to use it in a quilt. Reverse portions of a design, such as the direction of the stem in this block, to create a mirror image. Next, think about where you can repeat the motif in your quilt. Blocks, sashing, and borders are all places where you can repeat design motifs.*

Flight of Fancy

*M*ANY BALTIMORE ALBUM *quilts feature peacocks, and they are one of my favorite motifs. The graceful tail feathers on this example will allow your color imagination to run wild. Try using seven different hues, as I did, or choose seven gradations of a single color for a monochromatic look. For the leaves, combine five fabrics, blending them into a subtle shading of color the way an artist mixes paints on a palette.*

TECHNIQUES

- ✑ Making 1 template from multiple shapes (branches)
- ✑ Cutwork appliqué (branches)
- ✑ Chevron appliqué (leaves)
- ✑ Unit appliqué (peacock)
- ✑ Stitching beyond marked shapes (peacock and leaves)

FABRICS

- ✑ 11" square for background
- ✑ 11" square for branches
- ✑ 6" square for peacock's body
- ✑ 7 assorted 4" squares for peacock's tail feathers
- ✑ 5 assorted 1¼" x 12" strips for chevron leaf and striped leaves
- ✑ 17 assorted 2" squares for plain leaves

STITCHING THE CUTWORK BRANCHES

1. Trace the branches (page 79) onto freezer paper, connecting them into a single shape. This will create a complete branch and allow you some play with positioning the completed peacock unit later. Draw dashed lines to create bridges that will connect the narrow shapes. Connecting the branches will help keep them in position when you press the template onto the fabric.

2. Cut out the template and press it onto the branch fabric. Mark around the template, but do not mark around the bridge areas. Remove the freezer paper and layer the marked fabric over the background square. Stitch the branches, cutting the 3/16" seam allowances as you work your way around.

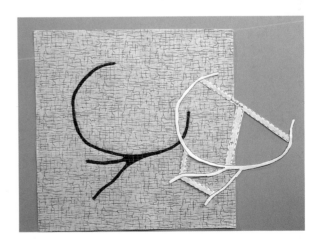

*A*LLOW SMALL IRREGULARITIES *in shape to occur as you stitch the branches to the background fabric. Slightly uneven branches will look natural.*

STITCHING THE PEACOCK

1. Trace the peacock (page 79) onto freezer paper, adding hatch marks where the tail feathers meet and where the peacock's body joins tail feather #1. These hatch marks indicate where to begin stitching successive tail feathers, and where to attach the innermost tail feather to the bird's body. Mark numbers 1–7 on the tail feather templates, and cut the templates apart.

2. Press tail-feather template #1 onto the appropriate fabric and mark around it. Include a hatch mark in the seam allowance that meets the one on the template. Cut a $^3/_{16}$" seam allowance around the tail feather. Clip into the seam allowance at the hatch mark, and stitch tail feather #1 to the tail feather #2 fabric, as shown. Begin stitching at the hatch mark, and continue stitching into the seam allowance just *beyond* the upper end of tail feather #1.

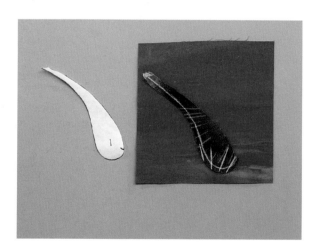

3. Press the template for tail feather #2 next to the previous line of stitching, aligning the hatch mark with the clip on tail feather #1. Mark around tail feather #2, adding a hatch mark in the seam allowance, as shown. Cut a $^3/_{16}$" seam allowance around tail feather #2.

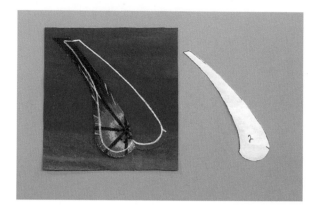

4. Stitch tail feather #2 onto the tail feather #3 fabric. Continue stitching in the same manner until all 7 tail feathers are joined. Stitch the inner side of tail feather #1 to the fabric for the peacock's body. Start stitching in the seam allowance at the top of tail feather #1, and end at the clip in the seam allowance of tail feather #1.

5. Press the template for the bird's body next to the stitched inner edge of tail feather #1, and mark around it. Remove the freezer paper and cut a $^3/_{16}$" seam allowance around the bird's body.

6. On the wrong side of the peacock unit, clip into the seam allowances between tail feathers, approximately ¼" from the top of each shape. Finger-press these short seam-allowance segments open to make it easier to stitch the peacock unit to the background fabric. Referring to the block photo (page 74) for placement, stitch the completed peacock unit on top of the branches.

ADDING THE LEAVES

1. Turn under and press a ¼" seam allowance on the darkest of your 1¼" x 12" strips of leaf fabric. Pin this strip to the next-lightest strip, matching the raw edge of the turned seam allowance to a long edge of the second strip. Stitch the first strip to the second. Press the joined strips flat.

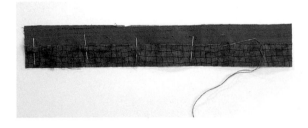

MACHINE STITCH 5 leaf strips together. Space each successive leaf ¼" from the previous one so that all 5 fabrics will show in your finished chevroned leaves.

2. Turn under and press the second fabric strip so that ¼" of it is visible above the previous line of stitching. Trim the turned-under seam allowance to ¼", and stitch the second strip to the third strip that is lighter than the second strip, as shown. Press the 3 joined strips. Continue adding strips in the same manner, working from darkest to lightest until all 5 strips are joined. Press the completed strips. Note that the first and the last strips will be wider than the others when finished. The wider strips allow you enough fabric to cut leaves in different color configurations.

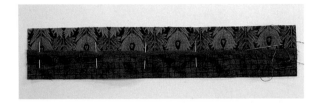

3. Trace one of the leaf patterns (page 79) onto template plastic, and cut it out. Place the template over the joined strips, and mark leaves in different configurations. For a true chevron effect, cut a half-leaf from template plastic and mark around it diagonally on the joined strips. Cut a ³/₁₆" seam allowance around the half-leaf; then appliqué the center seam of this leaf to the joined fabric strips in the opposite direction. Add a few stitches just beyond both points of the leaf for added security. Press the center seam allowance open. This will let the leaf lie flat and make it easier to stitch to the background square. Cut a ³/₁₆" seam allowance around the leaf.

4. To make a *half*-chevron leaf, mark around a half-leaf template on the joined strips. Cut out the half-leaf, leaving a 3/16" seam allowance. Stitch the center seam of the half-leaf to plain fabric, stitching a bit beyond the points for security. Mark around the half-leaf template on the plain fabric, as shown. Trim the center seam, leaving a 3/16" seam allowance, and cut a 3/16" seam allowance around the outside of the leaf. Press the center seam allowance open.

5. For plain leaves, trace a leaf shape (page 79) onto freezer paper. Mark, remove the freezer paper, and cut, leaving a 3/16" seam allowance.

6. Referring to the photo below for placement, stitch the leaves to the background fabric along the branches.

INSTEAD OF USING green for the chevron and striped leaves, consider echoing a hue you used in the peacock's tail feathers. Blue, pink, purple, rust, red, gold, or magenta—5 gradations of any color would make great chevron leaves.

Square Wreath

*T*HIS DESIGN REMINDS *me of an Asian house, with bamboo and colorful Chinese coins in each window. A white-on-white print in the center opening features delicate lines and swirls that resemble Japanese script, and the subtle background fabric echoes those shapes*

TECHNIQUES

- ⚬ Cutwork appliqué (wreath)
- ⚬ Unit appliqué (six-part background square)
- ⚬ Reverse appliqué (leaves)
- ⚬ Using a window template (leaves)
- ⚬ Broderie-perse appliqué (circles)

FABRICS

- ⚬ 11" square for outer background
- ⚬ 11" square for wreath
- ⚬ Print fabric with at least 12 assorted ¾" circle motifs*
- ⚬ 5 assorted 5" squares for background areas inside wreath
- ⚬ ⅛ yard multicolored print for inner leaves
- ⚬ 12 assorted 2" squares for outer leaves

The circles in the block photo (page 80) are ¾" finished, but slightly smaller or larger circles will also work well.

STITCHING THE CUTWORK WREATH

1. Trace the wreath pattern (page 85) onto freezer paper, and cut it out. Press the template onto the wreath fabric and mark around it. Remove the freezer paper.

2. Center the marked wreath fabric on top of the 5" background square you want to use in the wreath center, and pin. Cut a ³/₁₆" seam allowance inside the marked line, cutting only through the wreath fabric. Stitch the center opening of the wreath fabric to the background fabric, as shown, cutting 2" of seam allowance at a time. Trim the background fabric on the wrong side, leaving a ³/₁₆" seam allowance.

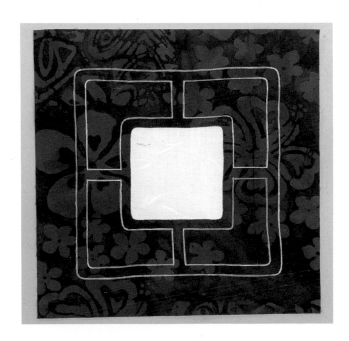

3. Stitch the remaining 4 wreath openings in the same manner. Use a different fabric for each opening. Trim the background fabrics underneath the block, leaving a 3/16" seam allowance.

You can stitch *the wreath to a single background fabric, or choose one print for the center opening, another for the surrounding openings, and a third for the outer background.*

4. Layer the square of wreath fabric over the square for the outer background, and pin. Referring to the block photo (page 80), stitch the outer edges of the wreath. Press the completed work.

Inside the final *line of stitching on the wrong side of the block, trim the outer background square to a ¼" seam allowance. This will reduce bulk in the finished block.*

Adding the Layered Leaves

1. Trace the scalloped leaf (page 85) onto freezer paper. Cut it out, leaving a window opening in the middle.

Make 4 freezer-paper *leaf templates instead of 1 to speed up the process of marking leaves on fabric.*

2. Place the leaf window-template on the outer-leaf fabric and mark around the inner and outer edges. Cut out the leaf, leaving 3/16" seam allowances inside and outside the leaf. Make 12 outer leaves.

3. Move the leaf window-template over the surface of the multicolored inner-leaf fabric until you find a color combination you like. Place a fabric leaf over this area, and stitch the inner edges in place. Repeat this process until you have stitched 12 leaves to the inner-leaf fabric. Trim the fabric on the wrong side, leaving a 3/16" seam allowance, and press the leaves.

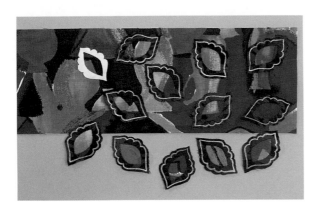

4. Referring to the block photo (page 80) for placement, stitch 4 layered leaves at each corner of the wreath. Start stitching each leaf near the innermost point to ensure that all 4 leaves will meet at the center.

5. To stitch the inner points of the scallops on each leaf, run a toothpick over the surface of a gluestick. Tuck under any stray threads that pop out at the inner point, and pinch the fabric to hold the threads in place while you continue stitching.

ADDING THE BRODERIE-PERSE CIRCLES

1. Cut 12 circles from the circle-motif print, leaving $3/16"$ seam allowances.

2. Referring to the photo for placement, appliqué a circle at the middle of the wreath's outer edge. Stitch another circle just inside each of the adjoining window openings to make a triangular formation. Repeat this process on the remaining sides of the wreath. The 12 stitched circles will create the illusion of an on-point square inside the wreath.

SCOPE OUT YOUR LOCAL QUILT SHOP *on a regular basis for fabrics that feature circular motifs. I've collected a couple of shelves full of great circles for broderie perse over the years, and I mix and match them for flower centers and for design elements like the Chinese coin–type circles in this block*

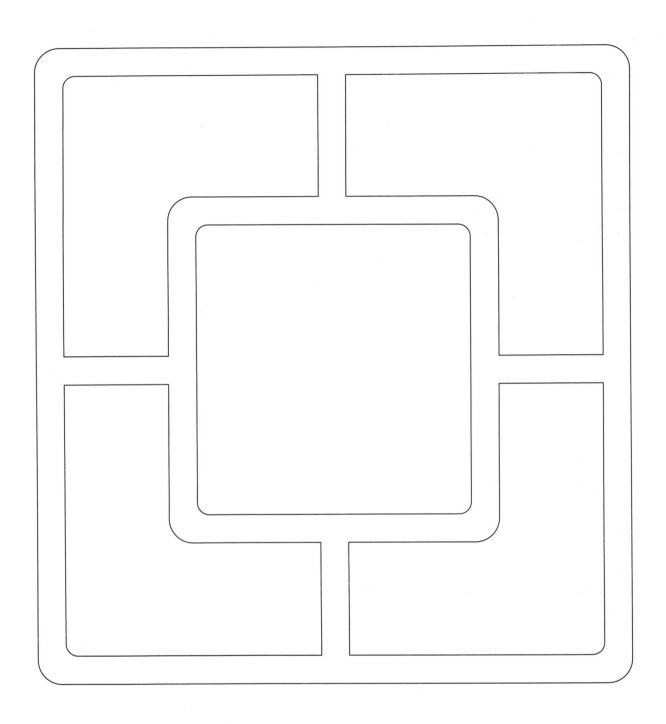

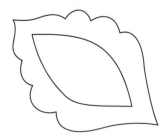

*T*HESE COLORFUL FLOWERS *look as though they've just been picked from a garden. Stitch them in a rainbow of summer colors, or alternate two hues in the tulips and choose a third for the middle flower. Your finished block will seem as bright and breezy as a summer day.*

TECHNIQUES

- ⚅ Scored turning lines (bias stems)
- ⚅ Permanent placement lines (background square)
- ⚅ Stitching bias strips to permanent placement lines (stems)
- ⚅ Unit appliqué (tulips)
- ⚅ No-template appliqué (tulip stripes)
- ⚅ Stitching beyond marked shapes (tulips)
- ⚅ Modified cutwork appliqué (center flower)
- ⚅ Reverse appliqué (large circle)
- ⚅ Broderie-perse appliqué (small circle)

FABRICS

- ⚅ 11" square for background
- ⚅ 5 assorted 6" squares for bias stems
- ⚅ 8 assorted 4" squares for tops and bottoms of tulips
- ⚅ 4 assorted 4" squares for tulip stripes
- ⚅ 4" square for middle flower
- ⚅ 4" square for large circle
- ⚅ 8 assorted 2" squares for leaves
- ⚅ Scrap with circular motif for broderie-perse circle
- ⚅ 3" x 4" piece for hand

PREPARING THE BACKGROUND SQUARE

USING a permanent (yes, *permanent*) fabric-marking pen or pencil, trace the stem placement lines (page 93) onto the background square. Because these lines are permanent, they will not smudge or bleed into the background fabric, and they will be completely covered after each stem is stitched. You won't need to soak water-soluble marks or wait to see if a misty cloud of blue will appear on the fabric later.

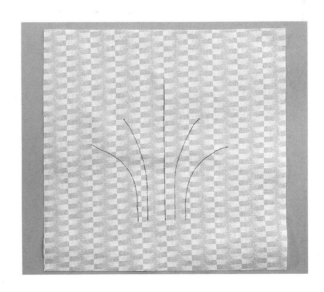

PREPARING PERFECT-BIAS STEMS

1. My method of making perfect-bias stems is super quick, easy, and produces precise, no-fail turning lines every time. Place a square of stem fabric on a cutting mat, with the *wrong* side facing up. Align the 45°-angle line on a quilter's ruler with the lower edge of the fabric and rotary cut the fabric diagonally into 2 triangles. Repeat for each square of stem fabric.

2. Lay a quilter's ruler over the cut edge of 1 triangle, aligning the ⅛" markings with the cut edge of the fabric. Hold the ruler firmly in place with your left hand, and place a hera marker next to the ruler. Slowly and firmly, move the hera back and forth across the fabric, pressing down very hard to score a straight line ⅛" from the cut edge of the fabric. Because you're working on the wrong side of the fabric, the ⅛" seam allowance you're creating will automatically turn in the right direction when you're ready to stitch the bias stem.

USE THIS PERFECT-BIAS technique for any appliqué design that features bias strips—it's great for vines, stems, stained glass quilts, and Celtic designs. The beauty of using a hera marker to score perfect turning lines and a rotary cutter to cut accurate seam allowances is that you can create perfectly precise, ready-to-stitch turning lines on bias strips of any width!

3. Move the ruler ¼" to the right, aligning the ¼" marks on the ruler with the first scored line. Using the hera, score a second line in the same way to produce 2 perfectly straight, parallel turning lines on the fabric.

4. Move the ruler ⅛" to the right of this second scored line, and rotary cut the fabric to complete the bias stem. Cut the short ends of the bias strip perpendicular to the long edges. Make 5 bias stems.

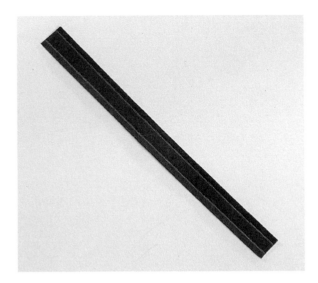

Consider using a color other than green for your stems. If leaves don't have to be green, neither do stems.

Stitching the Bias Stems

1. With raw edges facing down, align a folded edge of the center bias stem with the placement line on the background square. Stitch the middle bias stem in place, working from the bottom up for the first side and from the top down for the other side.

2. Following the directional stitching arrows on the pattern, stitch the 2 curved stems to the *right* of the center stem. Stitch the inner curves of each stem first; then stitch the opposite sides.

If you like, you can finger-press the scored lines on each of the bias stems to make the folds crisper.

3. For the 2 stems that lie to the *left* of the center stem, work from the top down and stitch the inner curves first. Then stitch the opposite side of these 2 stems. Follow the directional arrows on page 93 to stitch the remaining 3 stems.

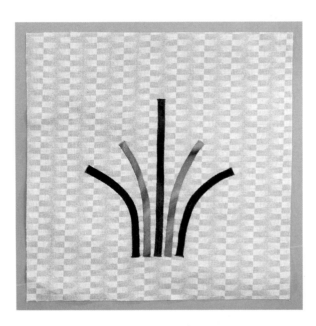

Stitching the Tulip

1. Trace a tulip (page 93) onto freezer paper, and cut it out. Press the template onto the tulip fabric and mark around it. Remove the freezer paper, and cut out the tulip, leaving a ³/₁₆" seam allowance. Make 4 tulips.

Choose similar color values for the middle flower and the 2 outer tulips. Making these 3 flowers in darker shades than the other flowers can help create visual balance.

2. Stitch the upper edge of a tulip to a piece of fabric for the tulip stripes, starting and ending your stitching just beyond the marked tulip. Using a 1" x 6" quilter's ruler, align the ⅛" marks on the ruler with the stitched line at the top of the tulip. Mark a line next to the ruler, stopping ⅛" from the next angle of the tulip. Continue marking around the upper edges of the tulip. Cut a ³⁄₁₆" seam allowance outside the marked lines. Trim the fabric underneath, leaving a ³⁄₁₆" seam al-lowance. Mark the short line at the sides of the tulip stripe by eye.

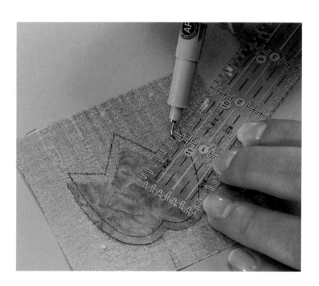

To ADD A *slight sheen, use silk douppioni for the tulip stripes and the large circle in the middle flower.*

3. Clip the seam allowance at the inner points of the tulip stripe, and stitch the tulip stripe to another square of tulip fabric. Mark the upper edge of the tulip unit as before.

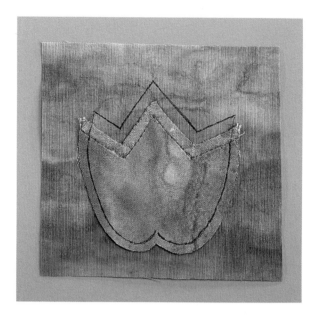

*J*UST FOR FUN, *try using a third fabric color for the top of the tulip unit.*

4. Cut a ³⁄₁₆" seam allowance around the top of the tulip unit. Trim the fabric underneath, leaving a ³⁄₁₆" seam allowance.

5. On the wrong side, clip into each of the seam allowances ¼" in from the edges of the tulip. Finger-press these short segments open to make the tulips easier to stitch to the background square.

6. Repeat steps 2–5 to complete 4 tulips. Referring to the block photo (page 86) for placement, stitch the 4 tulip units on top of the 4 outer curved bias stems.

STITCHING THE MIDDLE FLOWER

1. Trace the middle flower pattern (page 93) onto freezer paper, and cut it out. Press the template onto the middle flower fabric and mark around it. Remove the freezer paper. Cut out the flower, leaving a ³/16" seam allowance *except* between the petals. This modified form of cutwork makes it easy to stitch the small, reverse-appliqué circle and the deep inner points between petals.

2. Mark the outline of the large circle on the flower shape.

USE A CIRCLE stencil (page 13) to mark a perfect circle inside your middle flower template.

3. Cut a ³/16" seam allowance *inside* the marked circle, and reverse appliqué the circle to the large-circle fabric. Trim the fabric underneath, leaving a ³/16" seam allowance.

4. Cut out a circle motif from the print scrap, leaving a ³/16" seam allowance. Stitch the small circle to the large circle in the middle flower. Stitch the completed middle flower over the middle stem.

ADDING THE LEAVES

1. Trace one of the leaf patterns (page 93) onto template plastic and cut it out. Place the template on a leaf fabric and mark around it. Cut out the leaf, leaving a ³/16" seam allowance. Make 8 leaves.

ECHO YOUR FLOWER colors in your leaves by using an array of different values.

2. Referring to the photo, stitch the leaves to the stems in an arrangement that pleases you.

ADDING THE HAND

1. Trace the hand pattern (page 93) onto template plastic and cut it out. Place the template on the hand fabric and mark around it. Cut out the hand, leaving a 3/16" seam allowance.

2. Referring to the photo for placement, stitch the hand over the bottom edges of the stems.

LAY YOUR HAND on a white sheet of paper, and mark around it with a permanent pen. Close the wrist area with a curved or straight line. Reduce this drawing on a photocopy machine to 60 percent of its original size. Trace the hand onto template plastic, and appliqué it over the stems in this block.

THE HAND IN THIS BLOCK is a vibrant shade of pink-orange, which is a hand-painted, one-of-a-kind fabric from Skydyes (see "Resources" on page 141). For the hand in your block, you could use any color of the rainbow, such as magenta, purple, blue, yellow, or burgundy. Explore the possibilities of using prints for texture, too—there are some wonderful batiks available today that would give this block a very contemporary look.

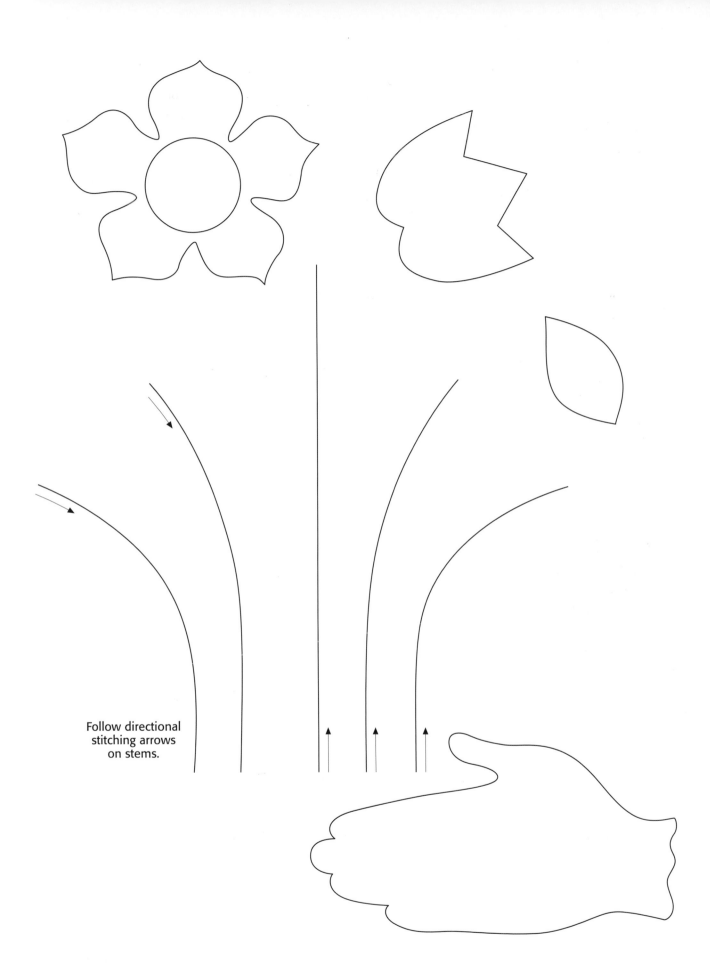

Follow directional
stitching arrows
on stems.

Dove and Dogwood Blossoms

*B*IRDS HAVE ALWAYS *been one of my favorite motifs for appliqué because there are so many different types, each with interesting curves and shapes. The double bands of color around this graceful dove create a clean, contemporary look. Fill the inner area with dogwood blossoms in warm colors, or choose blues and purples for a cooler look.*

TECHNIQUES

- Reverse appliqué (dove)
- No-template appliqué (outlines around dove and dogwood petals, scallops around pentagon)
- Unit appliqué (dove and dogwood blossoms)
- Modified cutwork appliqué (dogwood blossoms)
- Broderie-perse appliqué (circles)

FABRICS

- 11" square for background
- 11" square for inner area of dove
- 2 different 11" squares for color bands around dove
- 4 assorted 3" squares for dogwood blossoms
- 4 assorted 3" squares for contrasting petal openings and tips
- Small scrap for pentagon
- Small scrap for scallops around pentagon
- Small print scrap with circular motifs for broderie-perse circles

*F*OR THE BACKGROUND *fabric in this block, try using a variegated light blue batik rather than a solid-color fabric. The finished block would suggest a dove seen against a summer sky.*

STITCHING THE DOVE

1. Mark the center of the inner-area fabric by folding the square in half twice and finger-pressing the folds at the center. Trace the dove pattern (page 99) onto freezer paper, and cut it out. Press the template onto the fabric for the first color band, matching the centers. Mark around the template. Layer the marked fabric over the fabric for the inner area of the dove. Begin cutting a 3/16" seam allowance *inside* the marked lines, cutting only through the top layer of fabric. Reverse appliqué the dove shape to the lower layer, cutting and stitching about 2" of fabric at a time. Trim the inner-dove fabric underneath the block, leaving a 3/16" seam allowance.

2. Using a 1" x 6" ruler for accuracy, mark a dashed line 1/8" outside the stitched dove. Space these marks 1/4" to 1/2" apart.

3. Cut a 3/16" seam allowance outside the marked dashes. There is no need to first connect the dashes into a solid line; you'll be able to turn under the fabric by eye.

4. Stitch the dove unit to the fabric for the next color band, matching the centers. Trim the color band, leaving a 3/16" seam allowance. Mark dashed lines 1/8" outside the stitching, as shown.

5. Cut a 3/16" seam allowance outside the dashed lines.

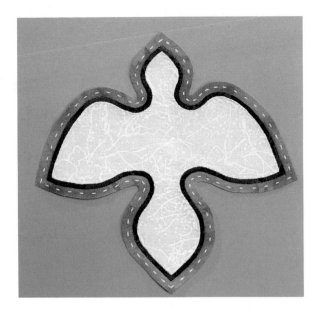

6. Referring to the block photo (page 94) for placement, stitch the second color band to the background fabric in the same manner as the first.

STITCHING THE DOGWOOD BLOSSOMS

1. Trace the dogwood blossom pattern (page 99) onto freezer paper, and cut it out. (Ignore the crossed lines on the pattern for now.) Press the template onto a dogwood fabric and mark around it. Remove the freezer paper and cut out the blossom, leaving a 3/16" seam allowance, except between petals. This modified form of cutwork will keep the petals perfectly placed as you stitch the openings and tips to a lower layer of fabric. Mark and cut 4 dogwood blossoms.

2. Referring to the dogwood blossom pattern, mark a straight line down the middle of each petal; then mark a short perpendicular line crossing the first, as shown, (just eyeball it). Pin a dogwood blossom to a piece of contrasting fabric, and cut into the dogwood fabric on both lines. Use a toothpick to turn under a smooth curve on each side of this opening, and give it a slight pinch to create a crisp fold, as you stitch the opening. Stitch the remaining openings in the same manner.

3. Trim the lower layer of fabric, leaving a 3/16" seam allowance.

4. Pin the dogwood blossom unit to another square of contrasting petal fabric that is either the same or a different color. In the upper portion of each petal, make a clip into the seam allowance on each side, spacing the clips differently from petal to petal. Stitch from clip to clip onto the square of contrasting petal fabric. To draw the tips of the petals, mark a curved line by eye on the contrasting fabric. There is no need to use a template for these curves; your dogwood blossoms will look more natural if they are not identical.

5. Cut a 3/16" seam allowance around each marked petal tip. Trim the fabric underneath, leaving a 3/16" seam allowance. Make 4 dogwood blossom units. Referring to the block photo for placement, stitch the dogwood blossoms inside the dove. Cut circular motifs from a print fabric, leaving a 3/16" seam allowance, and stitch a circle to the center of each dogwood blossom.

ADDING THE PENTAGON MOTIF

1. Trace the pentagon pattern (page 99) onto freezer paper, and cut it out. Press the template onto the pentagon fabric and mark around it. Remove the freezer paper and cut out the pentagon, leaving a 3/16" seam allowance. Stitch the pentagon to the scallop fabric. Mark curved scallops from point to point around the pentagon. Because the scallops are so small, it's easy to mark them by eye. Cut a 3/16" seam allowance around the scallops.

2. Using a circle stencil (page 13), mark and cut a very small circle motif from a print with circular motifs, leaving a 3/16" seam allowance. Stitch the circle to the center of the pentagon motif. Referring to the block photo (page 94) for placement, stitch the pentagon unit to the dove's head.

Delicate Dahlia

MOTHER NATURE IS *a never-ending source of great motifs for appliqué. Analyzing the color patterns in a real flower gave me the idea for connecting the inner petals of this dahlia into a single stitched shape and then cutting out the larger unit. The result is an easy-to-stitch flower with evenly spaced colors.*

TECHNIQUES

- ⚬ Cutwork appliqué (vine)
- ⚬ Unit appliqué (dahlia)
- ⚬ Making 1 template from multiple shapes (dahlia)
- ⚬ Marking a shape *after* stitching fabrics together (dahlia)
- ⚬ No-template appliqué (dahlia)
- ⚬ Broderie-perse appliqué (circle)

FABRICS

- ⚬ 11" square for background
- ⚬ 11" square for vine
- ⚬ 20 assorted 2" to 3" squares for leaves
- ⚬ Small print scrap for large circle
- ⚬ 5" square for inner petals
- ⚬ 8" square for middle petals
- ⚬ 8" square for outer petals
- ⚬ 4" square for stamens
- ⚬ Scrap with circular motifs for small broderie-perse circle

STITCHING THE VINE

1. Trace the vine pattern (pages 105–106) onto freezer paper, adding the bridge indicated by the dashed lines. Cut out the template and press it onto the vine fabric. Mark around the vine, but do not mark the bridge.

FOR YOUR VINE, *choose the complement color of your flower color. For example, if your flower is gold, make the vine purple, or if your flower is red, make the vine green.*

2. Remove the freezer paper, and lay the marked vine fabric on the background fabric. Referring to the block photo (page 100) for placement, stitch the vine in place, cutting and stitching approximately 2" of fabric at a time.

ADDING THE LEAVES

1. Trace the leaf patterns (page 100) onto freezer paper, and cut them out.

2. Mark and cut 20 leaves. Referring to the block photo (page 100) for placement, stitch the leaves along the vine.

STITCHING THE DAHLIA

1. Trace the inner petal shape (page 107) onto freezer paper, connecting the petals to form a single template. Mark the word "top" on the template, and cut out the template. Press it onto the inner-petal fabric and mark around it. Remove the freezer paper and cut out the inner petals, leaving a $3/16$" seam allowance. Stitch the inner-petal shape to the middle-petal fabric. Make your stitches as tiny as possible so that the fabrics will stay joined securely when you cut the petals later. Trim away the middle-petal fabric underneath, leaving a $3/16$" seam allowance.

2. Trace the middle petals (page 107) onto a piece of template plastic, and cut them out. Notice that the outer petal tips are *not* included in the pattern. Mark the word "top" on the template. Place this template over the stitched inner-petal shape, aligning the "tops." Mark around the middle petals.

3. Trace the stamen pattern (page 107) onto freezer paper, and cut it out. Press the template onto the stamen fabric and mark around it. Remove the freezer paper. Cut out the stamen, leaving a 3/16" seam allowance. Stitch the stamens onto the petal unit. Because the stamens are very narrow, it will be easy to adjust their positions slightly, if necessary.

4. Cut a 3/16" seam allowance around the middle petals.

5. At the top of each middle petal, make a clip into the seam allowance on each side, spacing the clips differently from petal to petal. Stitch from clip to clip onto the outer-petal fabric. Draw the curves of the outer-petal tips on the fabric by eye, starting at one end of the stitched line and ending at the other.

6. Cut a 3/16" seam allowance around each outer-petal tip. Trim the fabric underneath, leaving a 3/16" seam allowance.

7. On the wrong side of the completed dahlia unit, make a clip into the seam allowances on both sides of each petal, ½" from the top. Finger-press these short segments open. Referring to the block photo for placement, stitch the completed dahlia unit on top of the vine and leaves.

Adding the Circles

1. Using a circle stencil (page 13), mark a ⅞" circle on the large-circle fabric. Cut out the circle, leaving a 3/16" seam allowance. Stitch the circle over the stamens at the center of the dahlia.

2. Cut a small circular motif from the print scrap, leaving a 3/16" seam allowance. Referring to the photo, stitch the small circle over the larger circle at the center of the dahlia.

For the stamen shape in this block, I used a printed batik, with several colors and lots of color contrast in it. The varied colors give the stamens a more subdued look that creates less visual impact than the other shapes in this flower. For a bolder, more contemporary feel, make the stamens in a bright or a dark solid-color fabric that contrasts starkly with the colors in your dahlia.

Bridge

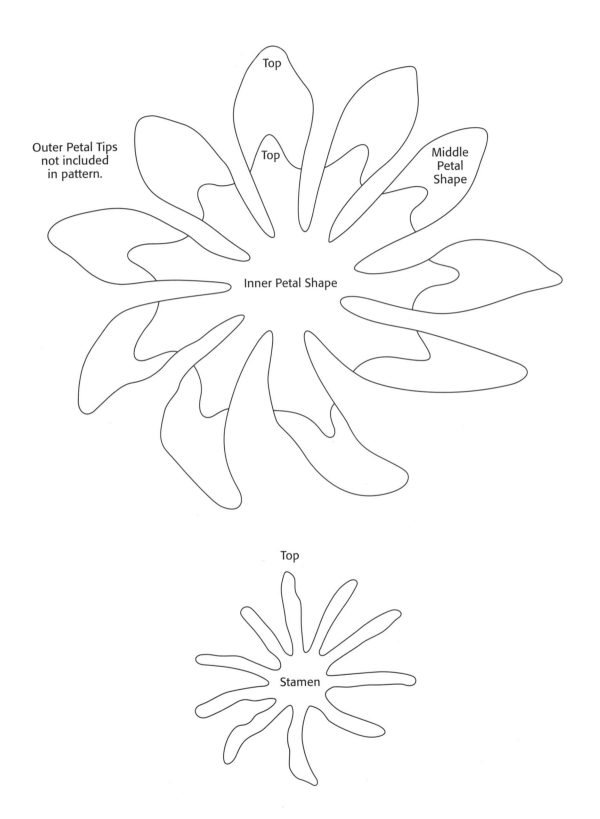

Top

Top

Outer Petal Tips
not included
in pattern.

Middle
Petal
Shape

Inner Petal Shape

Top

Stamen

M Y METHOD FOR *making perfect bias strips with a hera marker and rotary ruler makes it a breeze to cut and stitch bias strips in any width you like. The possibilities are limitless, from making super-simple stems like the ones in the Summer Nosegay block (page 86), to outlining flowers and leaves with narrow bands of color.*

TECHNIQUES

- Cutwork appliqué (stem)
- Scored turning lines (bias strips)
- Mitering acute angles (bias strips)
- Permanent placement lines (background square, leaves, and flower petals)

FABRICS

- 11" square for background
- 11" square for stem
- 9" x 18" piece for bias strips
- 3 assorted 3" squares for petal centers
- 3 assorted 3" squares for leaf centers

STITCHING THE STEM

1. Trace the stem pattern (page 113) onto freezer paper, and cut it out. Press the template onto the stem fabric and mark around it. Remove the freezer paper.

2. Referring to the block photo (page 108) for placement, stitch the stem to the background fabric, working with about 1" to 2" of fabric at a time. On both sides of the stem, end the stitching about 1" before you reach the calyx.

PREPARING THE BIAS STRIPS

1. Place the fabric for the bias strips on a cutting mat, with the wrong side up. Align the 45°-angle line on a 3" x 18" quilter's ruler with the lower edge of the fabric, and use a rotary cutter to cut the fabric diagonally.

2. Align the ⅛" marks on the ruler with the cut edge of the fabric, and place a hera marker next to the ruler. Pressing down very hard, slowly move the hera across the fabric. This will score a straight, easy-to-see turning line exactly ⅛" from the cut edge of the fabric.

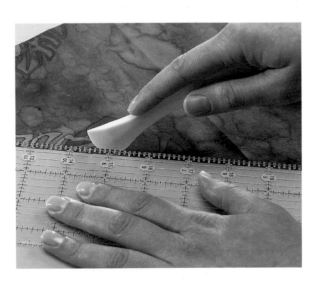

3. Move the ruler ⅛" to the right of the first scored line. Using the hera in the same manner, score a second line. Move the ruler ⅛" to the right of the second scored line, and rotary cut the other edge of the bias strip. Rotary cut the short ends of the bias strip perpendicular to the long edges.

4. You now have a perfect ⅛"-wide bias strip, with scored lines that will automatically turn in the right direction. Finger-press the scored lines to make the folds crisper. Make 6 of these bias strips.

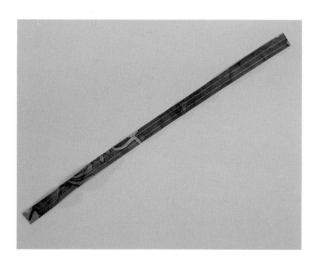

Make each of *the bias strips a different color, or choose one color for outlining the leaves and another for outlining the petals.*

STITCHING THE LEFT LEAF

1. Trace the darkened lines of the left-leaf pattern (page 113) onto freezer paper. This will be the first stitching line. Cut out the template, cutting the curved line *into* the template. Press the template onto the leaf fabric. Mark around the template, gently lifting the freezer paper up to mark the curved line inside the leaf. You'll stitch the fold of a bias strip to these marked lines, covering them.

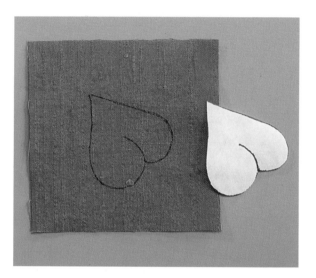

2. With raw edges facing down, align a fold of a bias strip with the leaf's inner curved line, extending the stem at least ⅛" beyond the line. Referring to the directional stitching arrows on the pattern, stitch the bias strip to the marked line, stopping at the leaf's point.

3. Fold the bias strip back on top of itself. Enough of the folded bias strip must extend beyond the

leaf point that it allows the needle to lie straight from the point of the leaf to the corner of the folded bias strip. Position the needle and bias strip until it looks like the photo. This process will show you exactly where the finished mitered seam will be. If necessary, make adjustments in the folded bias strip.

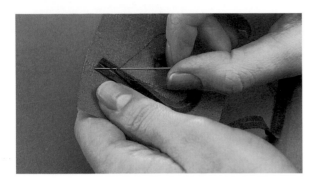

4. When you're satisfied with the position of the bias strip, pinch a sharp crease in the fold. Take a stitch through both folds of the bias strip, anchoring them to the leaf point. Turn the folded bias strip to the left, creating a mitered fold that goes straight out from the leaf point.

5. Stitch this closed, starting at the leaf point as shown, and finishing at the edge of the bias strip.

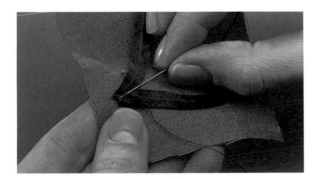

6. Stitch the bias strip to the next side of the leaf, stopping underneath the bias strip where the first stitching began. Trim the excess bias strip, checking to make sure the first part will overlap the final portion.

7. Trim the bias strips underneath the mitered point, leaving a 3/16" seam allowance. Open the short seam allowance under the mitered seam, and finger-press it flat.

8. Trim the leaf fabric underneath the leaf unit, leaving a 3/16" seam allowance. Referring to the block photo (page 108) for placement, stitch the left leaf over the left stem. Use a toothpick to gently tuck under the point and corners of the bias strip as you work.

Stitching the Right Leaves

1. The 2 leaves on the right side of the stem are mirror images of the left leaf. Make these leaves in the same manner as the left leaf, referring to the directional stitching arrows on the pattern.

2. Referring to the block photo (page 108) for placement, stitch the 2 right leaves in place on the right stems.

Stitching the Flower Petals

1. Trace the bottom-left petal pattern (page 113) onto freezer paper, and cut it out. This is the line for stitching the bias strip to the petal fabric. Press the template onto the petal fabric and mark around it.

2. Stitch a bias strip to the petal fabric. Start stitching at one leaf point, leaving ½" of the bias strip free. When you reach the other point, miter the seam as you did for the leaves. Trim the bias strip underneath the mitered seam, leaving a 3/16" seam allowance. Open it and finger-press it flat. Trim the petal fabric, leaving a 3/16" seam allowance. Make 3 flower petals.

3. Overlap the 3 flower petals, and stitch them together. Trim the excess fabric underneath each leaf, leaving a 3/16" seam allowance.

4. Pin the calyx over the lower edge of the joined petals, and stitch it to the petal unit. Stitch the petals and calyx to the background fabric.

Make the tips *of your petals rounded rather than pointed.*

Petal

SOMETIMES APPLIQUÉ DESIGNS *are related to patchwork cousins. In this block, I used double bias strips and flowers to give a new twist to the classic Dresden Plate.*

TECHNIQUES

- Unit appliqué (flower petals and center circle)
- Hand piecing (flower petals)
- Scored turning lines (double bias strips and flower petals)
- Permanent placement lines (small background square and double bias strips)
- Stitching bias strips to permanent placement lines (center circle)
- Broderie-perse appliqué (flower centers)

FABRICS

- 11" square for block background
- 4" square for center-circle background
- 1" x 12" bias strip of light fabric for center circle
- 1" x 12" bias strip of dark fabric for center circle
- 1 light fabric, cut into sixteen 3" x 4" pieces for Dresden petals
- 16 assorted 3" x 4" dark fabrics for Dresden petals
- 3" square for stem
- 3 assorted 2" squares for flowers
- 6 assorted 1" squares for leaves
- Print scrap with three ¼" circle motifs

STITCHING THE PETAL UNITS

1. Trace the Dresden petal pattern (page 119) onto template plastic, and cut it out. Note that both the top and angled edges *include* a ¼" seam allowance, while the long, straight edge does *not*. Mark the words "right side" on your template so that it will be easy to remember where the center seam is.

2. Mark around the template on a piece of light fabric. Mark another line ⅛" out from the long, straight edge. This line adds the seam allowance for joining the light half of the petal to the dark fabric. Cut out the petal directly on the marked lines.

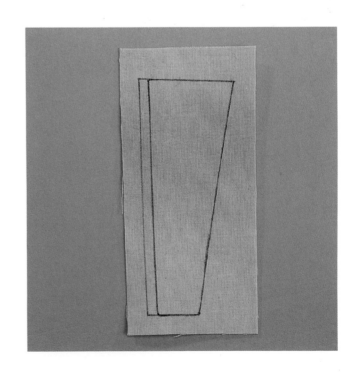

3. Turn under and finger-press the ⅛" seam allowance. Stitch this edge to a dark petal fabric. Place the petal template on the fabric next to the stitched seam, aligning edges, and mark around it.

4. Cut out the dark half of the petal on the marked lines, trimming the fabric underneath even with the seam allowance of the light half. Finger-press this seam allowance open. On top of a cutting mat, fold the petal right sides together and use a hera marker to score a stitching line ¼" from the upper edge. Using a #10 or #11 Sharp needle, hand piece the top edges of each petal together with short running stitches, starting at the seam line and working outward.

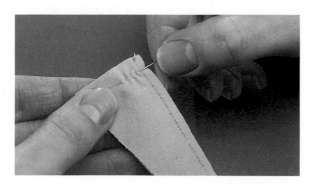

5. Turn the petal right side out, creating a point at the top. Press the petal so that it lies flat. Make 16 Dresden petals, each with a light fabric in the right half and a dark fabric in the left.

6. Place 2 petal units right sides together, and hand piece the angled edges. Continue joining petals as shown, until you have a complete circle with 16 petals.

7. Fold the block background in half twice and finger-press the folds; then fold and finger-press the circular petal unit in the same manner. Place the petal unit on top of the block background, matching the horizontal and vertical creases. Stitch the outer points of the petals to the 11" background square, leaving the inner edges unstitched.

STITCHING THE DOUBLE BIAS STRIPS

1. Lay the light 1" x 12" bias strip on a cutting mat, with the right side facing up. Use a ruler and permanent pen to mark a straight line down the center.

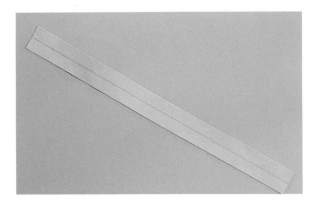

2. Place the dark 1" x 12" bias strip on a cutting mat, with the wrong side up. Lay a ruler ⅛" over the cut edge, and use a hera marker to score a turning line. Move the ruler ⅛" to the right of the scored turning line, and score a second turning line. Move the ruler ⅛" to the right, and rotary cut the fabric. Trim the short ends of this bias strip perpendicular to the long edges.

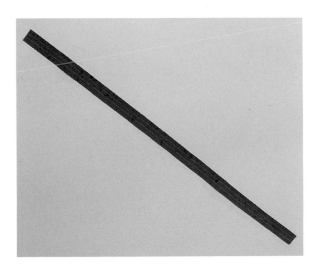

3. Stitch the dark strip to the marked line on the light bias strip. Make your stitches tiny, for security.

4. Place the stitched bias strips on a cutting mat, wrong sides up. Trim the seam allowance of the light bias strip even with the seam allowance of the dark strip. Use a ruler and a hera marker to score a turning line on the light strip, ⅛" from the stitching.

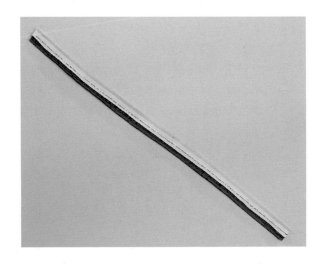

Stitching the Center Circle

1. Using the circle stencil (page 119) and a permanent pen, mark a 2½" circle on the 4" background square.

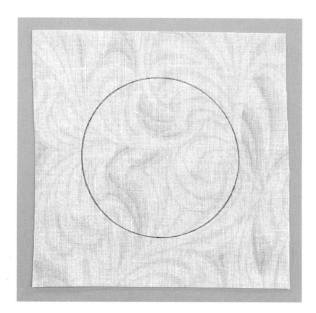

2. Stitch the double bias strip to the marked circle, with the light fabric on the inside. Finish by folding under the end of the bias strip, and overlapping and stitching the fold to the beginning of the double bias strip. Trim the background fabric underneath and the ends of the bias strips, leaving a ³/₁₆" seam allowance. Finger-press the turning line all the way around the outer edge of the dark bias strip.

3. Referring to the block photo (page 114) for placement, stitch the center-circle unit over the inner edges of the Dresden flower petals. On the wrong side of the block, trim the background fabric, leaving a ³/₁₆" seam allowance.

4. Trace the small flowers, leaves, and stem (page 119) onto freezer paper, and cut them out. Press the templates onto the flower, leaf, and stem fabrics, and mark around them. Remove the freezer paper, and cut out each shape, leaving a ³/₁₆" seam allowance. Referring to the photo, appliqué these shapes to the center circle, covering the seam in the double bias strips with one of the flowers or leaves. Cut ¼" circle motifs from the print scrap, adding ³/₁₆" seam allowances, and stitch one of the circles to each flower.

2½" Circle

Add ⅛" seam allowance to this edge.

Right side

Hummingbird and Trillium

*A*PPLIQUÉING PARTIAL SEAMS *is a wonderful way to create multifabric backgrounds, and it's easier than you might think. In this block, all you need to do is add one background fabric at a time under two overlapping vines. It's so much fun, you may find yourself thinking about other ways to use this technique.*

TECHNIQUES

- 🌀 Unit appliqué (bird)
- 🌀 Partial seams (overlapping vines)
- 🌀 Reverse appliqué (trillium)
- 🌀 Matching multiple points (trillium)

FABRICS

- 🌀 10" square for lower-left background
- 🌀 4" x 10" piece for upper-left background
- 🌀 4" x 10" piece for upper-right background
- 🌀 4" x 10" piece for lower-right background
- 🌀 4" x 10" piece for horizontal vine
- 🌀 5" x 10" piece for vertical vine
- 🌀 9 assorted 2" squares for trillium petals
- 🌀 9 assorted 2" squares for contrasting petal openings
- 🌀 4" square for bird's body
- 🌀 Two 3" squares for bird's wings

MARKING THE VINES

1. Trace the horizontal vine pattern (page 126) onto freezer paper; include the lines that indicate the outside edges of the background square. Cut out the template and press it onto the vine fabric. Mark around the outer edge of the vine.

2. Remove the freezer paper and cut away the inner edge of the horizontal vine template. Press the template back onto the fabric and mark the other side of the vine. Remove the freezer paper, and cut a $^3/_{16}$" seam allowance outside the marked lines.

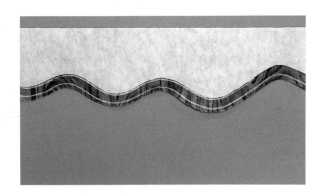

3. Mark and trim the fabric for the vertical vine in the same manner.

STITCHING THE OVERLAPPING VINES

1. Layer the marked horizontal vine fabric over the lower-left background fabric. Place the marked vertical vine fabric over the horizontal vine, and insert a straight pin at the point where the 2 vines overlap. Mark a small hatch mark in the seam allowance of the horizontal vine to indicate how far to stitch it to the lower-left background fabric.

2. Stitch the horizontal vine to the lower-left background fabric, stopping at the hatch mark.

3. Layer the vertical-vine fabric over the partially stitched horizontal vine, and stitch it to the lower-left background fabric, beginning slightly inside the stitched horizontal vine. Trim the background fabric underneath, and both sides of the vine, as shown.

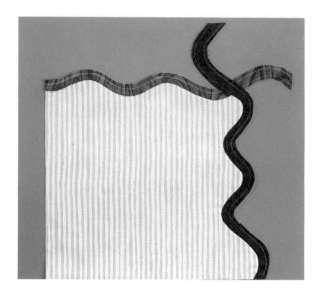

4. Layer the unit from step 3 over the upper-left background fabric and stitch the other side of the horizontal vine in place. Also stitch the remaining portion of the vertical vine, starting at the edge of the block. Trim the upper-left background fabric underneath, as shown.

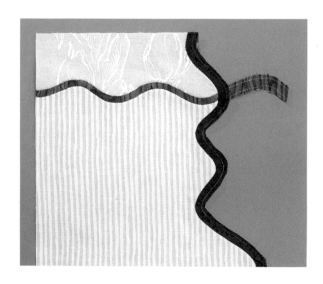

5. Layer the unit from step 4 over the upper-right background fabric. Starting at the edge of the block, stitch the upper portion of the horizontal vine. Stitch the vertical vine, starting slightly inside the horizontal vine and ending at the edge of the block. Trim the upper-right background fabric underneath, in the same manner as before.

6. Layer the unit from step 5 over the lower-right background fabric. Stitch the final portion of the horizontal vine, ending at the edge of the block. Stitch the final portion of the vertical vine, ending at the hatch mark. Trim the lower-right background fabric underneath, as before. Press the completed background square to prepare it for stitching the trillium petals and bird.

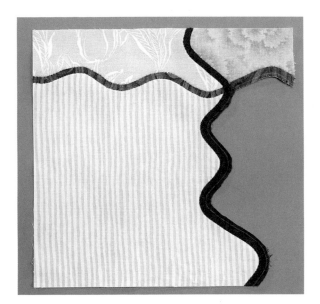

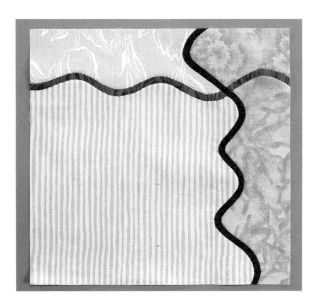

You can use this overlapping vine technique in the borders of a quilt, as well as in blocks.

STITCHING THE TRILLIUM

1. Trace a trillium petal (page 126) onto template plastic, and cut it out. Mark 9 trillium petals on the trillium fabric.

2. Mark 3 slightly curved lines inside each trillium petal. Use the lines on the pattern pieces as guides, or simply mark the lines freehand. The narrow openings do not need to be identical from petal to petal.

IF YOU WANT the petals in this design to look like leaves, omit the stitched openings and scatter more leaves over the vines. There are no rules about leaf or petal placement, so let your creativity flow and stitch them wherever you like.

3. Cut out a trillium petal, leaving a 3/16" seam allowance, and lay it on top of a piece of contrasting fabric. Cut the middle line marked on the petal. Use a wooden toothpick to turn under a very narrow seam allowance, and stitch the middle petal opening, shaping a curve at the ends of the marked line. Repeat this process for the remaining openings. Trim the contrasting fabric underneath, leaving a 3/16" seam allowance. Stitch all 9 petals in the same manner.

MATCHING PETAL POINTS

1. Making petal points come together perfectly is easy—all you need to do is focus on the points themselves and let the outer areas of the petals fall where they will. Start by stitching 1 petal to a vine so that the point touches the vine.

2. To add a second petal, start by turning under and finger-pressing the fold on one side of the second petal so that it will be easy to position the folded edge accurately beside the first stitched petal. Pin the folded seam allowance of the second petal to the background fabric, carefully aligning the folded petal point with the point of the stitched petal. Make sure that the unfolded adjacent edge of the second petal slightly overlaps the vine. This way, when you turn under a fold on the edge of the second petal, there will be enough fabric at the point to make any slight adjustments necessary for petals that meet perfectly.

3. Stitch the second petal point, tugging the thread slightly at the point. Take a stitch to anchor the point so that it matches the first petal point. Turn under the seam allowance along the next side and finish stitching the second petal.

4. Follow the same process to stitch the third petal, matching it to the first 2 petal points. When all 3 petals are stitched, the eye will notice how beautifully the inner points meet, rather than the distance between the outer petal points.

STITCHING THE BIRD

1. Trace the bird's body, including the dashed lines (page 126), onto freezer paper and cut it out. Press the template onto the body fabric and mark around it. Remove the freezer paper, and cut out the body, leaving a ³/₁₆" seam allowance.

2. Trace a complete wing pattern (page 126) onto freezer paper, and cut it out. Press the template onto the wing fabric and mark around it. Remove the freezer paper, and cut out the wing, leaving a ³/₁₆" seam allowance. Repeat this step for the second wing.

3. Stitch the wings to the bird's body, starting and ending your stitching just inside the marked lines of the bird's body.

4. Referring to the block photo below for placement, stitch the bird unit onto the lower-left background.

Stitch a hummingbird close to a trillium petal so that it looks as though the bird is tugging on the petal. Or add 2 or 3 birds, instead of just 1. Place them wherever you like inside the lower-left background area.

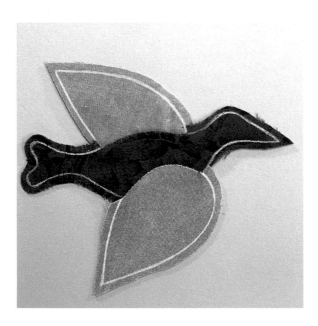

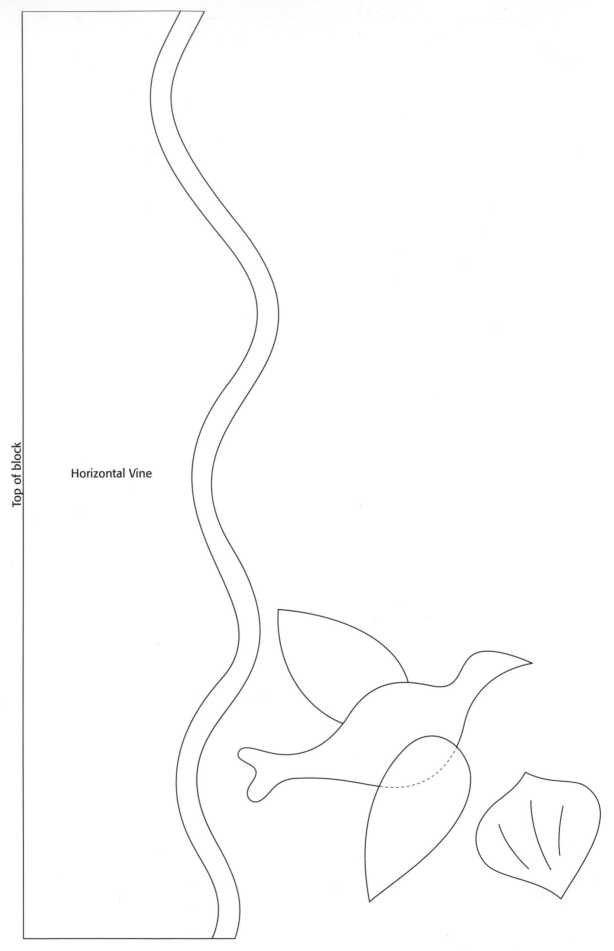

Top of block

Horizontal Vine

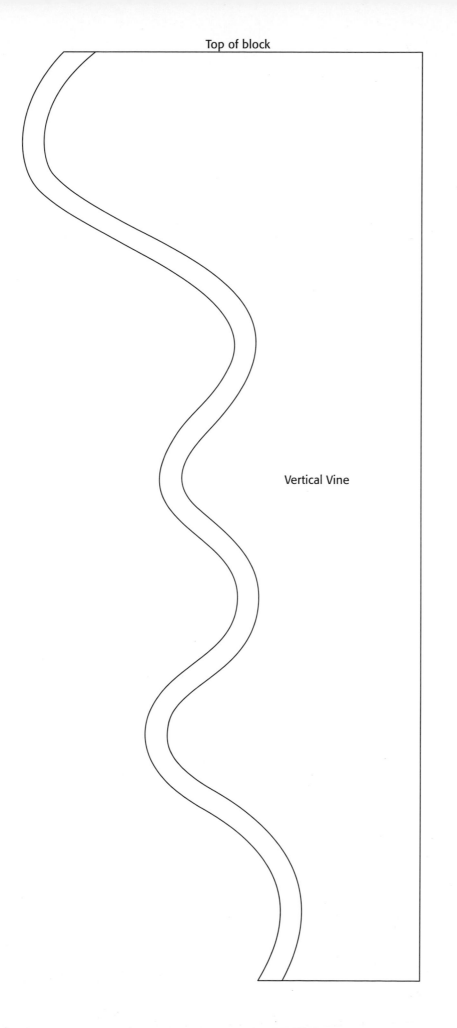

Top of block

Vertical Vine

Top of block

*A*FTER APPLIQUÉING THIS *star, perfect points will be at your fingertips. You'll be able to tackle anything from gentle tips to steep points.*

TECHNIQUES

- ❀ Unit appliqué (entire star)
- ❀ No-template appliqué (long star points)
- ❀ Broderie-perse appliqué (center circle motif)

FABRICS

- ❀ 11" square for background
- ❀ 9" square for long star points (use tightly woven fabric only)
- ❀ 8" square for short points
- ❀ 8" square for area between short and long points
- ❀ 4" square for medium star points around center circle
- ❀ Scrap of print fabric with 2½" circle motif

STITCHING THE STAR UNIT

1. Trace the center points pattern (page 133) onto freezer paper, adding a ³/₁₆" seam allowance, and cut it out. Press the template onto the fabric for the medium points around the center circle, and mark around it. Remove the freezer paper. Stitch the medium points onto the fabric for the long star points. Trim the long-point

fabric underneath, leaving a ³/₁₆" seam allowance. Lay a 1" x 12" ruler over the stitched medium points, so that the ruler lies over 2 opposite points. Mark a dot 2" from the tip of each point, as shown in the lower-left photo.

2. Mark lines from each dot to either side of the stitched points to create the long star points, without templates. Repeat this process around the star.

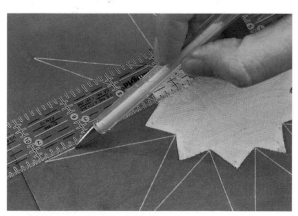

3. Cut a $3/16$" seam allowance around each long point. Layer the partially stitched star unit over the fabric for the area between the points. Stitch the large star points to this fabric, stitching about $1\frac{1}{4}$" on each side. Trim the fabric underneath the center area, leaving a $3/16$" seam allowance. Trace the cone shape (page 133) onto template plastic, and cut it out. Mark around the outer edges of the template, between the long star points.

*F*OR BEST RESULTS, *use a batik for the long star points in this block. Batiks have a closer weave than some fabrics, and they won't fray as easily in very small areas such as these star points.*

4. Cut a $3/16$" seam allowance around the marked curves between points, and stitch these curves to the fabric for the short points. Trim the fabric underneath, leaving a $3/16$" seam allowance. Trace the short-point shape (page 133) onto freezer paper, and cut it out. Mark the short points all the way around the star.

5. Referring to the block photo, stitch the short points to the background fabric. Trim the fabric underneath, leaving $3/16$" seam allowance.

Completing the Long Points

1. To make sure that each long point will stay arrow-straight, finger-press the sides to create a crisp fold. Stitch to the tip of the first long point, keeping your needle in the fabric as you take the last stitch. Trim some of the fabric in the seam allowance underneath to reduce bulk.

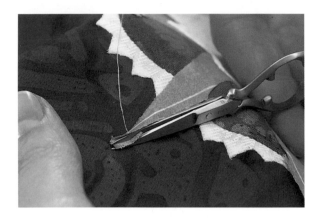

2. Bring your needle out of the fabric and use a wooden toothpick to turn under a fold at the tip of the point.

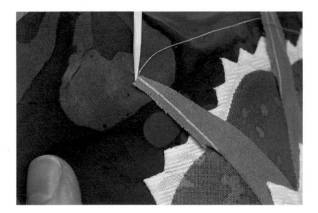

Take a stitch to anchor the folded tip onto the background square. I actually take a second stitch on top of the first, for added security. Keep both stitches tiny.

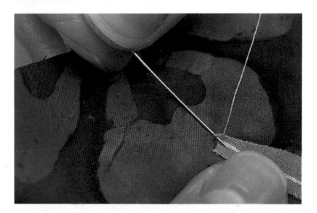

3. Trim the seam allowance on the next side of the point to reduce bulk. If you're working with a batik or other tightly woven fabric, you'll be able to trim the fabric to ⅛" from the marked seam line. Use a wooden toothpick to turn under the seam allowance from the tip of the point to about ½" along the next side of the point. When you're happy with the way the fabric lies, run a toothpick over the top of a water-soluble gluestick, and tuck a bit of glue under the seam allowance. Pinch the fabric between your fingers to hold it in place while you stitch the remaining portion of the point.

Stitching the Center Circle

Cut a 2½" circle motif from the print fabric, leaving a ³/₁₆" seam allowance, and stitch it on top of the medium points. Refer to the block photo for placement.

To use a fabric *without printed motifs, mark a 2½" circle on a piece of fabric. If you take this approach, consider adding a couple of smaller circles to the center.*

For the center *circle in this star, try using some machine embroidery stitches. Many sewing machines are capable of stitching decorative motifs in many different sizes. Experiment on scrap fabric until you find a design that pleases you. Stitch the design onto a piece of fabric, and then use a circle template to mark a circle around the completed motif.*

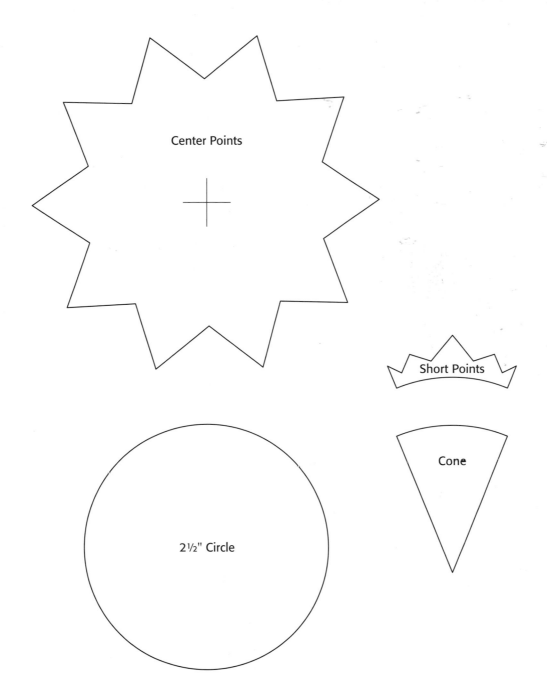

Center Points

Short Points

Cone

2½" Circle

VIBRANT ORANGES, PINKS, *purples, and yellows give this lily a luminous quality. The leaves create interesting positive-negative images—the spaces between the leaves are as interesting as the leaves themselves.*

TECHNIQUES

- ⚘ Unit appliqué (lily and 3-part background)
- ⚘ Cutwork appliqué (stem)
- ⚘ Overlapping appliqué shapes (stem and fence post)
- ⚘ Scored turning lines (fence post)

FABRICS

- ⚘ 11" square for left-hand background
- ⚘ 2" x 11" strip for fence post
- ⚘ 11" square for right-hand background
- ⚘ 11" square for stem
- ⚘ Assorted 2" and 3" squares for lily unit
- ⚘ 22 assorted 2" squares for leaves

STITCHING THE STEM AND FENCE POST

1. Trace the stem pattern (page 139) onto freezer paper, including the dashed lines of the bridge and the area where the fence post overlaps the stem. Cut out the template and press it onto the stem fabric. Mark around the template (but not around the bridge), making small hatch marks in the seam allowance where the fence post will overlap the stem. Remove the freezer paper.

2. Layer the marked stem fabric over the fabric for the left background. Following the directional stitching arrows on the pattern, stitch the lower portion of the stem and cut a $3/16$" seam allowance around the upper stem, as shown in the photo at right.

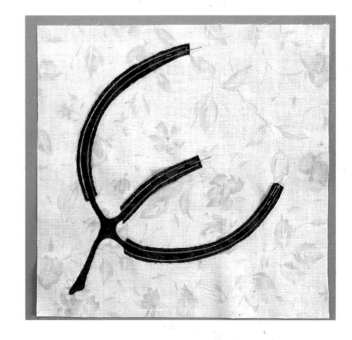

3. For the fence post, cut a 1¼" x 11" strip of fabric and use a hera marker to score turning lines ⅛" from each long edge. Stitch the left edge of the fence post over the stem. Trim away the excess background fabric, as shown.

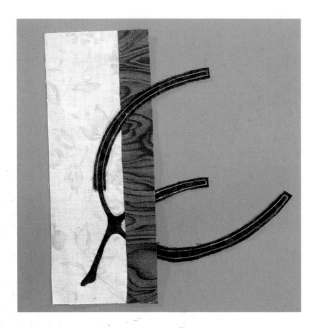

4. Pin the stem-and-fence post unit onto the right-hand background fabric and stitch the 2 lower stems. Stitch the right edge of the fence post over the lower stems, and stitch the upper stem over the fence post.

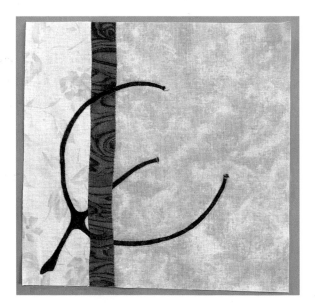

STITCHING THE LILY UNIT

1. Trace the complete lily pattern (page 138) onto freezer paper, including the numbers. The same number is used on petals consisting of 2 or 3 parts. For example, the first petal unit contains 2 pieces, both labeled with a *1*. Stitch the smaller of these 2 pieces onto a piece of petal fabric, and mark the outline of the petal around it. Press the templates for petals 2 and 3 next to marked petal #1, and make a small hatch mark in the seam allowance of petal #1 where it joins petals #2 and #3.

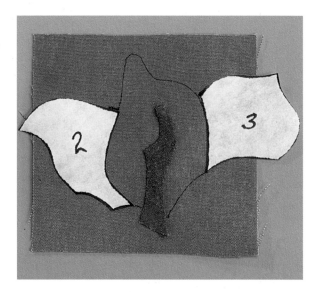

2. Cut out petal unit #1, leaving a 3/16" seam allowance *except* along the lower edge, where a 1/4" seam allowance is needed for overlap. Stitch the left edge of petal #1 onto the fabric for petal #2, starting your stitching at the hatch mark. Mark around the template for petal #2 as shown.

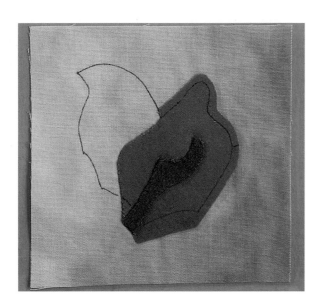

3. Cut out petal #2, leaving a 3/16" seam allowance except along the bottom, where you'll add a 1/4" seam allowance, as before. Stitch the right edge of petal unit #1 to the fabric for petal #3, as before, and mark petal #3 as shown.

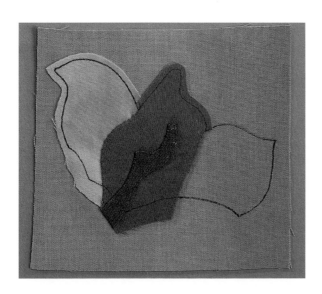

4. Cut a 3/16" seam allowance around petal #3, leaving a larger seam allowance around the lower edge as before. This completes the top section of the lily. Stitch together the pieces for petals #4, #5, and #6 in the same manner.

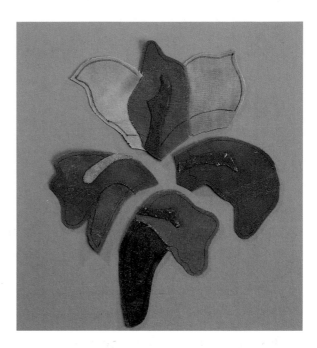

5. Referring to the block photo (page 138) for placement, stitch all of the petal units to the block to complete the lily.

ADDING THE LEAVES

1. Trace a leaf pattern (page 138) onto template plastic, and cut it out. Mark around the template on each of the leaf fabrics. Cut out each leaf, leaving a 3/16" seam allowance. Make 22 leaves.

2. Referring to the block photo (page 134), stitch the leaves along the stems.

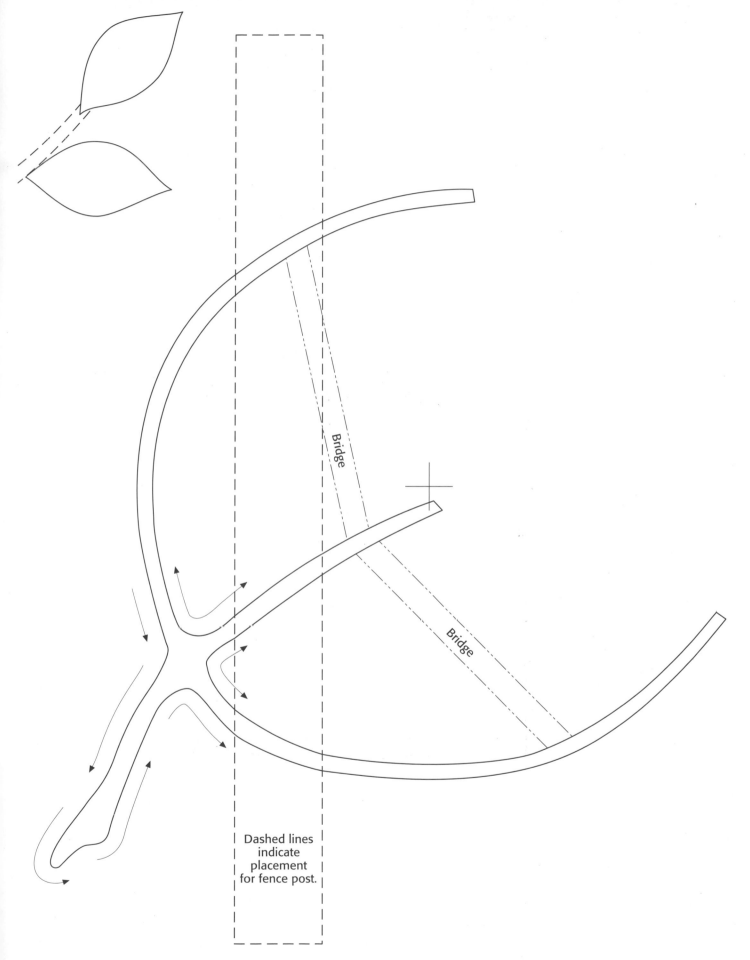

Bridge

Bridge

Dashed lines
indicate
placement
for fence post.

Resources

Mickey Lawler's Skydyes
P.O. Box 370116
West Hartford, CT 06137-0116
e-mail: Skydyes@aol.com
Website: www.skydyes.com
Fax: 860-236-9117
Hand-painted cottons and silks, fabric paints

Jeana Kimball's Foxglove Cottage
P.O. Box 698
Santa Clara, UT 84765
e-mail: FoxgloveCottage@worldnet.att.net
Size #11 Straw Needles

Mulberry Silk & Things
P.O. Box 150
Rocheport, MO 65279-0150
800-854-2726
E-mail: mulberrysilk@juno.com
Web site: www.mulberrysilk.com
Size #12 Sharp needles

Salem Manufacturing Co., Inc.
170 Braided Blanket Bluff
Alpharetta, GA 30022-7030
770-521-7983
Fax: 770-664-7679
E-mail: salemrule@msn.com
Mitering rulers, rotary-cutting equipment

The Summer House Needleworks
6375 Oley Turnpike Rd.
Oley, PA 19547
610-689-9090
Fabrics and block-of-the-month kits

About the Author

JANE TOWNSWICK is an accomplished author, editor, quilter, teacher, and former shop owner who has developed amazing expertise in appliqué. She has been featured as a guest artist and instructor at Elly Sienkiewicz's esteemed Appliqué Academy, and her work has been praised in *American Quilter* and *Quilter's Newsletter* magazine. Jane lives, teaches, and quilts in Allentown, Pennsylvania.

Photo by John Hamel

Martingale & Company
Toll-free: 1-800-426-3126

International: 1-425-483-3313
24-Hour Fax: 1-425-486-7596

PO Box 118, Bothell, WA 98041-0118 USA

Web site: www.patchwork.com
E-mail: info@martingale-pub.com

Books from

These books are available through your local quilt, fabric, craft-supply, or art-supply store. For more information, contact us for a free full-color catalog. You can also find our full catalog of books online at www.patchwork.com.

Appliqué
Appliqué for Baby
Appliqué in Bloom
Baltimore Bouquets
Basic Quiltmaking Techniques for Hand Appliqué
Basic Quiltmaking Techniques for Machine Appliqué
Coxcomb Quilt
The Easy Art of Appliqué
Folk Art Animals
Fun with Sunbonnet Sue
Garden Appliqué
The Nursery Rhyme Quilt
Red and Green: An Appliqué Tradition
Rose Sampler Supreme
Stars in the Garden
Sunbonnet Sue All Through the Year

Beginning Quiltmaking
Basic Quiltmaking Techniques for Borders & Bindings
Basic Quiltmaking Techniques for Curved Piecing
Basic Quiltmaking Techniques for Divided Circles
Basic Quiltmaking Techniques for Eight-Pointed Stars
Basic Quiltmaking Techniques for Hand Appliqué
Basic Quiltmaking Techniques for Machine Appliqué
Basic Quiltmaking Techniques for Strip Piecing
The Quilter's Handbook
Your First Quilt Book (or it should be!)

Crafts
15 Beads
Fabric Mosaics
Folded Fabric Fun
Making Memories

Cross-Stitch & Embroidery
Hand-Stitched Samplers from I Done My Best
Kitties to Stitch and Quilt: 15 Redwork Designs
Miniature Baltimore Album Quilts
A Silk-Ribbon Album

Designing Quilts
Color: The Quilter's Guide
Design Essentials: The Quilter's Guide
Design Your Own Quilts
Designing Quilts: The Value of Value
The Nature of Design
QuiltSkills
Sensational Settings
Surprising Designs from Traditional Quilt Blocks
Whimsies & Whynots

Holiday
Christmas Ribbonry
Easy Seasonal Wall Quilts
Favorite Christmas Quilts from That Patchwork Place
Holiday Happenings
Quilted for Christmas
Quilted for Christmas, Book IV
Special-Occasion Table Runners
Welcome to the North Pole

Home Decorating
The Home Decorator's Stamping Book
Make Room for Quilts
Special-Occasion Table Runners
Stitch & Stencil
Welcome Home: Debbie Mumm
Welcome Home: Kaffe Fassett

Knitting
Simply Beautiful Sweaters
Two Sticks and a String

Paper Arts
The Art of Handmade Paper and Collage
Grow Your Own Paper
Stamp with Style

Paper Piecing
Classic Quilts with Precise Foundation Piecing
Easy Machine Paper Piecing
Easy Mix & Match Machine Paper Piecing
Easy Paper-Pieced Keepsake Quilts
Easy Paper-Pieced Miniatures
Easy Reversible Vests
Go Wild with Quilts
Go Wild with Quilts—Again!
It's Raining Cats & Dogs
Mariner's Medallion
Needles and Notions
Paper-Pieced Curves
Paper Piecing the Seasons
A Quilter's Ark
Sewing on the Line
Show Me How to Paper Piece

Quilting & Finishing Techniques
The Border Workbook
Borders by Design
A Fine Finish
Happy Endings
Interlacing Borders
Lap Quilting Lives!
Loving Stitches
Machine Quilting Made Easy
Quilt It!
Quilting Design Sourcebook
Quilting Makes the Quilt
The Ultimate Book of Quilt Labels

Ribbonry
Christmas Ribbonry
A Passion for Ribbonry
Wedding Ribbonry

Rotary Cutting & Speed Piecing
101 Fabulous Rotary-Cut Quilts
365 Quilt Blocks a Year Perpetual Calendar
All-Star Sampler
Around the Block with Judy Hopkins
Basic Quiltmaking Techniques for Strip Piecing
Beyond Log Cabin
Block by Block
Easy Stash Quilts
Fat Quarter Quilts
The Joy of Quilting
A New Twist on Triangles
A Perfect Match
Quilters on the Go
ScrapMania
Shortcuts
Simply Scrappy Quilts
Spectacular Scraps
Square Dance
Stripples Strikes Again!
Strips That Sizzle
Surprising Designs from Traditional Quilt Blocks

Traditional Quilts with Painless Borders
Time-Crunch Quilts
Two-Color Quilts

Small & Miniature Quilts
Bunnies by the Bay Meets Little Quilts
Celebrate! With Little Quilts
Easy Paper-Pieced Miniatures
Fun with Miniature Log Cabin Blocks
Little Quilts all Through the House
Living with Little Quilts
Miniature Baltimore Album Quilts
A Silk-Ribbon Album
Small Quilts Made Easy
Small Wonders

Surface Design
Complex Cloth
Creative Marbling on Fabric
Dyes & Paints
Fantasy Fabrics
Hand-Dyed Fabric Made Easy
Jazz It Up
Machine Quilting with Decorative Threads
New Directions in Chenille
Thread Magic
Threadplay with Libby Lehman

Topics in Quiltmaking
Bargello Quilts
The Cat's Meow
Even More Quilts for Baby
Everyday Angels in Extraordinary Quilts
Fabric Collage Quilts
Fast-and-Fun Stenciled Quilts
Folk Art Quilts
It's Raining Cats & Dogs
Kitties to Stitch and Quilt: 15 Redwork Designs
Life in the Country with Country Threads
Machine-Stitched Cathedral Windows
More Quilts for Baby
A New Slant on Bargello Quilts
Patchwork Pantry
Pink Ribbon Quilts
Quilted Landscapes
The Quilted Nursery
Quilting Your Memories
Quilts for Baby
Quilts from Aunt Amy
Whimsies & Whynots

Watercolor Quilts
More Strip-Pieced Watercolor Magic
Quick Watercolor Quilts
Strip-Pieced Watercolor Magic
Watercolor Impressions
Watercolor Quilts

Wearables
Easy Reversible Vests
Just Like Mommy
New Directions in Chenille
Quick-Sew Fleece
Variations in Chenille

5/00